WESTKNITS
BESTKNITS

NUMBER 1 - SHAWLS

Stephen West

Patterns and Instructions
STEPHEN WEST

Page Layout and Book Design
NANCY MARCHANT

Copyright © 2016 by Stephen West

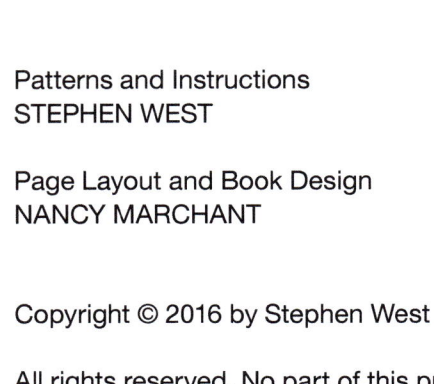

All rights reserved. No part of this publication may be reproduced or used in any form or by any means–graphic, electronic, or mechanical, including photocopying, recording, or information storage-and-retrieval systems–without written permission of the author.

The written instuctions, photographs, designs, projects and patterns are intended for the personal, noncommercial use of the retail purchaser and are under copyright laws; they are not to be reproduced in any form for commercial use. Permission is granted to photocopy patterns for the personal use of the retail purchaser.

West, Stephen, 1988-
Westknits Bestknits: Number 1 - Shawls
152 pages
ISBN/EAN: 978-0-9851317-6-0

FIRST EUROPEAN EDITION

CONTENTS

Introduction Stephen West	4
Exploration Station	6
Dotted Rays	16
The Doodler	30
Vertices Unite	48
Striped Bolting	58
Starburst	68
Color Craving	82
Askews Me Shawl	92
Knit 'n Slide	102
Garter Breeze	110
Boardwalk	120
Holey Chevrons	128
Briochevron Wrap	136
Abbreviations	146
Credits	148
Contact information	151

Stephen West

My first knitting pattern was a simple triangular shawl in 2009 called Boneyard Shawl and I haven't stopped knitting shawls and scarves since then. I love how they start so small and quickly grow into beautiful fabric as I add textured stitch patterns or rhythmic increases. The repetitive rows and motifs feel like a little dance as I'm knitting. I began creating scarves to use small amounts of hand dyed sock yarn and wore them like kerchiefs to go with my jeans and plaid wardrobe in the corn fields of Urbana, Illinois. Soon after I started designing knitwear I moved to Amsterdam in 2010 to study choreography at the arts school which allowed me to experiment with movement and expand my creative boundaries. I was surrounded by a completely new environment and began traveling to new countries, soaking up colorful inspiration in each place with Iceland as a frequent and favorite destination. I feel like my six years studying, living, and traveling through Europe was one big residency that fostered a drastic style evolution in my designs. I've blossomed into a brighter, more splashy color palette and discovered new artists and designers that have inspired me like Walter van Beirendonck.

Photoshoot days are my favorite because the knitted shawls finally come to life with styling and makeup. WESTKNITS BESTKNITS Number 1 - Shawls features several talented photographers with photos taken from 2013-2016. Alexandra Feo was the first photographer I collaborated with in Amsterdam. Her artistic work and personal style has been an enormous inspiration to me. I am always amazed by her precision and attention to detail. She manages to capture an entire fantasy in each photo while still focusing on the knitted item. Alexandra is an equally talented makeup artist as well. Our work together in 2013 and 2014 sparked a colorful shift in my approach to style and design.

This book is filled with my favorite shawl designs. The sign of a good shawl for me is when I can't stop knitting and upon finishing, I immediately cast on and knit the same shawl with new colors. I love re-knitting my designs with fresh color combinations to satisfy my color cravings that coordinate with fashionable outfits. My favorite element of knitting and fashion is color so I always encourage knitters to add a color pop to their projects. I think about all my designs as playgrounds or coloring books for experimenting with color. I show my interpretation of each design, but I love when knitters change and modify the design, making it their own. I don't believe in many color rules when it comes to multi-color striped projects. I make very instinctual choices and if I love a color, I just use it. If I don't feel like the colors are working, I don't rip out my knitting. Instead, I add more color until the fabric explodes with harmonious and clashing combinations. Remember, more is more and less is a bore when knitting Westknits patterns.

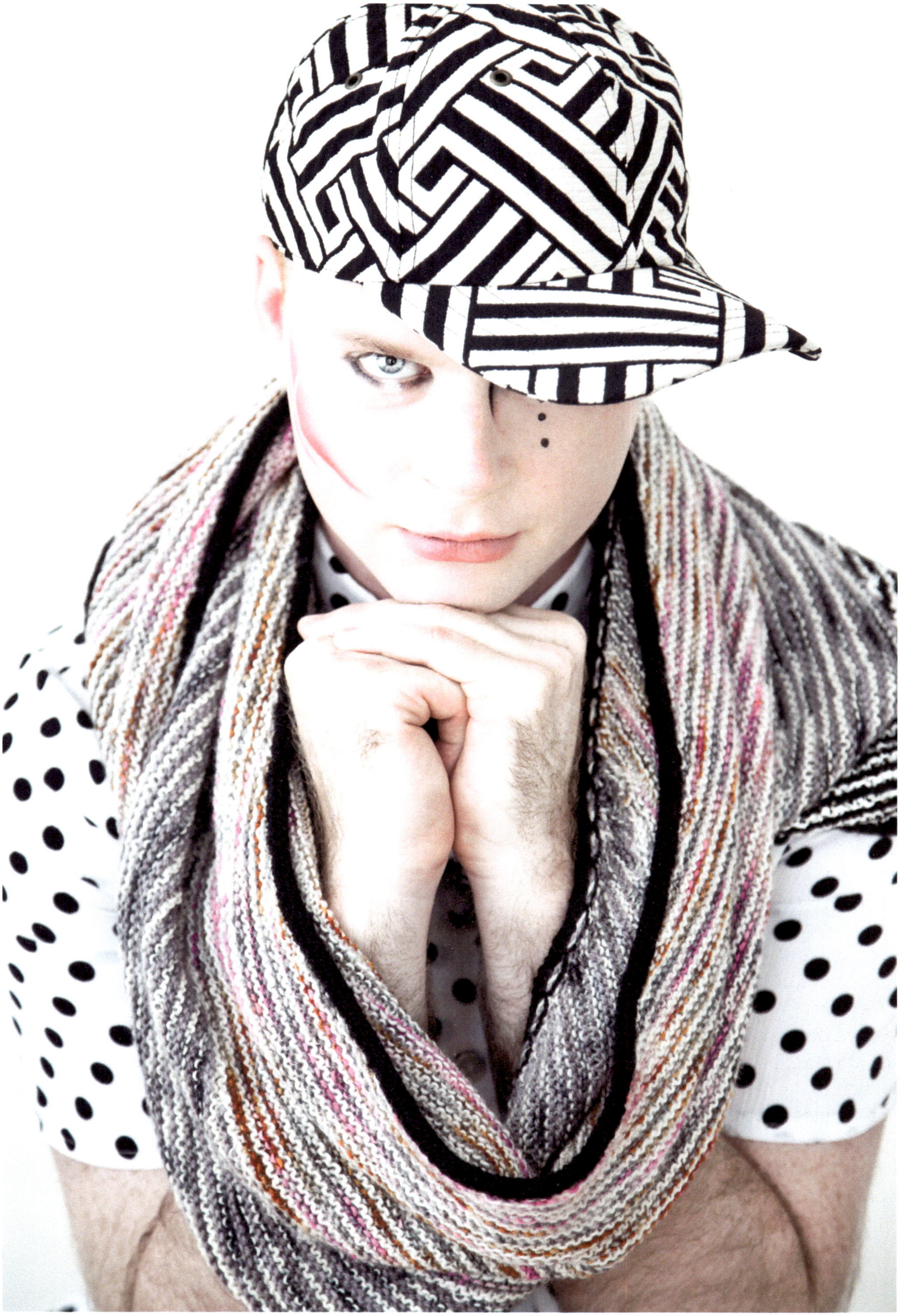

EXPLORATION
STATION

7

EXPLORATION STATION

This semi-circular shawl starts with an I-cord cast on and increases with short rows and yarn overs in the first section. Two color brioche forms the next section followed by slipped stitches and textured stripes. The final chevron border features a pop of color and an I-cord bind off. Choose 4 colors and enjoy the Exploration Station!

Finished Measurements: 22" / 56cm from CO to BO, 70" / 178cm wingspan length. Measurements taken after blocking.

Yarn: Fingering weight

Shown in: Neutral/Neon Peach Version
Madelinetosh Tosh Merino Light (100% Merino Wool; 420yds / 384m per 115g skein)
A - Thunderstorm
B - Neon Peach
C - Dusk
D - Antler

Purple Version
Hedgehog Fibres Sock Yarn (90% Merino, 10% Nylon; 437yds / 400m per 100g skein)
Color A - Spell
Colors B, C & D - Crystal, Granny, Naive, Opalite, Hush
The purple sample shows 5 contrast colors instead of 3. Change colors as you wish and combine them however you like.

Yardage: Color A - 275yds / 251m
Color B - 200yds / 183m
Color C - 185yds / 169m
Color D - 260yds / 238m

Needles: 40" US 6 / 4mm circular

Notions: Tapestry needle

Gauge: 20 sts & 48 rows = 4" / 10cm in garter stitch

Use these video tutorials to assist with Sections 1 & 2:
www.youtube.com/watch?v=8YTvU5jxG34
www.youtube.com/watch?v=LcTLmuWdpvU

9

INSTRUCTIONS
SECTION 1 - Shortrow Showdown

Using A, CO 3 sts with a long tail CO, *slip 3 sts to left needle, k3, repeat from * 4 more times. You should now have an I-cord 5 rows long. Do not slip sts to left needle after knitting the last 3 sts. Pick up and k3 sts along the edge of I-cord.

Next Row (WS): K3 CO sts, k3, sl3 wyif. 9 sts.

Row 1 (RS): K4, (yo twice, k1) twice, sl3 wyif.
Row 2 (WS): K4, (k1/p1 into double yo, k1) twice, sl3 wyif. 13 sts.

Row 3 (RS): K10, sl3 wyif.
Row 4 (WS): K10, sl3 wyif.

Repeat last 2 rows once more.

Row 7 (RS): K4, (yo twice, k1) 6 times, sl3 wyif.
Row 8 (WS): K4 (k1/p1 in to double yo, k1) 6 times, sl3 wyif. 25 sts. Break color A.

Wedge 1
Row 1 (RS): Using B, k3, kfb, k16, turn to work WS.
Row 2 (WS): K to last 3 sts, sl3 wyif.

Row 3 (RS): K3, kfb, k to 3 sts before last turn, turn to work WS.
Row 4 (WS): K to last 3 sts, sl3 wyif.

Repeat last 2 rows 6 more times. Break color B. 33 sts.

Next Row (RS): Using A, k3, kfb, k1, (ssk, yo twice, k1) 8 times, k1, sl3 wyif.
Next Row (WS): K3, kfb, k1, (k1/p1 into double yo, k2) 8 times, k2, sl3 wyif. 43 sts. Do NOT break color A.

Wedge 2
Row 1 (RS): Slip 8 sts to right needle. Using C, k to last 3 sts, sl3 wyif.
Row 2 (WS): K3, kfb, k to last 8 sts (in other words, k all C sts), turn to work RS row.

Row 3 (RS): K to last 3 sts, sl3 wyif.
Row 4 (WS): K3, kfb, k to 4 sts before last turn, turn to work RS row.

Row 5 (RS): K to last 3 sts, sl3 wyif.
Repeat last 2 rows 9 more times. 54 sts. Break color C.
Slide stitches over to the other needle to work another RS row with color A.

Next Row (RS): Using A, k3, kfb, k4, (yo twice, k2tog, k2) 10 times, yo twice, k2tog, k1, sl3 wyif.
Next Row (WS): K3, kfb, k1, (k1/p1 into double yo, k3) 11 times, k3, sl3 wyif. Break color A. 67 sts.

Wedge 3
Row 1 (RS): Using D, k3, kfb, k to last 7 sts, turn to work WS.
Row 2 (WS): K to last 3 sts, sl3 wyif.

Row 3 (RS): K3, kfb, k to 5 sts before last turn, turn to work WS.
Row 4 (WS): K to last 3 sts, sl3 wyif.

Repeat last 2 rows 12 more times. Break color D. 81 sts.

Next Row (RS): Using A, k3, kfb, k3, (ssk, yo twice, k3) 14 times, k1, sl3 wyif.
Next Row (WS): K3, kfb, k3, (k1/p1 into double yo, k4) 14 times, k2, sl3 wyif. 97 sts. Do NOT break color A.

Wedge 4
Row 1 (RS): Slip 10 sts to right needle. Using B, k to last 3 sts, sl3 wyif.
Row 2 (WS): K3, kfb, k to last 10 sts (in other words, k all B sts), turn to work RS row.

Row 3 (RS): K to last 3 sts, sl3 wyif.
Row 4 (WS): K3, kfb, k to 6 sts before last turn, turn to work RS row.

Row 5 (RS): K to last 3 sts, sl3 wyif.
Repeat last 2 rows 15 more times. 114 sts.

Break color B.
Slide stitches over to the other needle to work another RS row with color A.

Next Row (RS): Using A, k3, kfb, k6, (yo twice, k2tog, k4) 16 times, yo twice, k2tog, k3, sl3 wyif.
Next Row (WS): K3, kfb, k3, (k1/p1 into double yo, k5) 17 times, k3, sl3 wyif. Break color A. 133 sts.

Wedge 5
Row 1 (RS): Using C, k3, kfb, k to last 9 sts, turn to work WS.
Row 2 (WS): K to last 3 sts, sl3 wyif.

Row 3 (RS): K3, kfb, k to 7 sts before last turn, turn to work WS.
Row 4 (WS): K to last 3 sts, sl3 wyif.

Repeat last 2 rows 18 more times. Break color C. 153 sts.

Next Row (RS): Using A, k3, kfb, k5, (ssk, yo twice, k5) 20 times, k1, sl3 wyif.
Next Row (WS): K3, kfb, k5, (k1/p1 into double yo, k6) 20 times, k2, sl3 wyif. 175 sts. Do NOT break color A.

Wedge 6
Row 1 (RS): Slip 12 sts to right needle. Using D, k to last 3 sts, sl3 wyif.
Row 2 (WS): K3, kfb, k to last 12 sts (in other words, k all D sts), turn to work RS row.

Row 3 (RS): K to last 3 sts, sl3 wyif.
Row 4 (WS): K3, kfb, k to 8 sts before last turn, turn to work RS row.

Row 5 (RS): K to last 3 sts, sl3 wyif.
Repeat last 2 rows 21 more times. 198 sts. Break color D.
Slide stitches over to the other needle to work another RS row with color A.

Next Row (RS): Using A, k3, kfb, k8, (yo twice, k2tog, k6) 22 times, yo twice, k2tog, k5, sl3 wyif.
Next Row (WS): K3, kfb, k5, (k1/p1 into double yo, k7) 23 times, k3, sl3 wyif. Break color A. 223 sts.

SECTION 2 - Bountiful Brioche
This section is worked using two-color brioche. Each row is worked twice, first with color B and then again with color C.

Row 1 (RS): Using B, k3, (k1, sl1yo) to last 4 sts, k1, sl3 wyif. Do not turn, slide stitches to work the same row with the other color.
Row 1 (RS): Using C, sl3 wyib, (sl1yo, brp1) to last 4 sts, sl1yo, sl3 wyib. Turn work to WS.

Row 2 (WS): Using B, k3, (brp1, sl1yo) to last 4 sts, brp1, sl3 wyif. Do not turn, slide stitches to work the same row with the other color.
Row 2 (WS): Using C, sl3 wyif, (sl1yo, brk1) to last 4 sts, sl1yo, sl3 wyif. Turn work to RS.

Row 3 (RS): Using B, k3, brkyobrk, (sl1yo, brk1) to last 5 sts, sl1yo, brkyobrk, sl3 wyif. Do not turn, slide stitches to work the same row with the other color. 4 sts increased.
Row 3 (RS): Using C, sl3 wyib, sl1yo, p1, (sl1yo, brp1) to last 6 sts, sl1yo, p1, sl1yo, sl3 wyib. Turn work to WS.

Row 4 (WS): Using B, k3, (brp1, sl1yo) to last 4 sts, brp1, sl3 wyif. Do not turn, slide stitches to work the same row with the other color.
Row 4 (WS): Using C, sl3 wyif, (sl1yo, brk1) to last 4 sts, sl1yo, sl3 wyif. Turn work to RS.

Row 5 (RS): Using B, k3, (brk1, sl1yo) to last 4 sts, brk1, sl3 wyif. Do not turn, slide stitches to work the same row with the other color.
Row 5 (RS): Using C, sl3 wyib, (sl1yo, brp1) to last 4 sts, sl1yo, sl3 wyib. Turn work to WS.

12

Row 6 (WS): Using B, k3, (brp1, sl1yo) to last 4 sts, brp1, sl3 wyif. Do not turn, slide stitches to work the same row with the other color.
Row 6 (WS): Using C, sl3 wyif, (sl1yo, brk1) to last 4 sts, sl1yo, sl3 wyif. Turn work to RS.

Repeat Rows 3-6 twice more, then repeat Rows 3 & 4 once more. There should be 16 knit column stitches on each side. 239 sts. Break colors B & C.

Next Row (RS): Using A, k3, (brk1, k1) 5 times, *yo twice, (brk1, k1) 4 times, brk1, yo twice, (k1, brk1) 4 times, k1, repeat from * 11 more times, yo twice, (brk1, k1) 3 times, brk1, sl3 wyif.
Next Row (WS): K10, (k1/p1 into double yo, k9) 25 times, k1, sl3 wyif. 289 sts. Break color A.

SECTION 3 - Sassy Slips
Carry colors C & D along the right edge while striping colors.

Row 1 (RS): Using D, k3, kfb, k to last 3 sts, sl3 wyif.
Row 2 (WS): K3, kfb, (k1, p1) to last 4 sts, k1, sl3 wyif.

Row 3 (RS): Using C, k3, kfb, (sl1 wyib, k1) to last 3 sts, sl3 wyif.
Row 4 (WS): K3, kfb, (k1, p1) to last 4 sts, k1, sl3 wyif.

Repeat last 4 rows 5 more times, then repeat Rows 1 & 2 once more. 315 sts. Break colors C & D.

Next Row (RS): Using color A, k3, kfb, k1, (k11, yo twice) 27 times, k10, sl3 wyif.
Next Row (WS): K3, kfb, k9, (k1/p1 into double yo, k11) 27 times, k3, sl3 wyif. 371 sts. Break color A.

SECTION 4 - Nothing but Knit
Row 1 (RS): Using color B, k3, kfb, k to last 5 sts, kfb, k1, sl3 wyif. Do not turn to work WS. Slide sts to work the same side with color D.
Row 2 (RS): Using color D, k to last 3 sts, sl3 wyif. Turn to work WS.
Row 3 (WS): Using color B, k3, kfb, k to last 5 sts, kfb, k1, sl3 wyif. Do not turn to work RS. Slide sts to work the same side with color D.
Row 4 (WS): Using color D, k to last 3 sts, sl3 wyif. Turn to work RS.

Repeat last 4 rows 5 more times. 395 sts. Break colors B & D.

Next Row (RS): Using color A, k3, kfb, k6, pm, k7, yo twice, (k13, yo twice) 28 times, k7, pm, k4, sl3 wyif.
Next Row (WS): K3, kfb, k3, slm, k7, (k1/p1 into double yo, k13) 28 times, k1/p1 into double yo, k7, slm, k8, sl3 wyif. 455 sts.

SECTION 5 - Chevron Shenanigans
Row 1 (RS): Using color A, k3, kfb, k to m, slm, ssk, k6, (yo twice, k6, SK2P, k6) 28 times, yo twice, k6, k2tog, slm, k to last 3 sts, sl3 wyif.
Row 2 (WS): K3, kfb, k to m, slm, k7, (k1/p1 into double yo, k13) 28 times, k1/p1 into double yo, k7, slm, k to last 3 sts, sl3 wyif.

Repeat last 2 rows 7 more times. 471 sts.

BO all sts on the next RS row using an I-cord BO as follows, *K2, k2tog tbl, slip 3 sts back onto left needle, repeat from * to last 3 sts. 6 total sts remain. Graft the 6 remaining sts together.

FINISHING
Weave in ends and block the finished shawl.

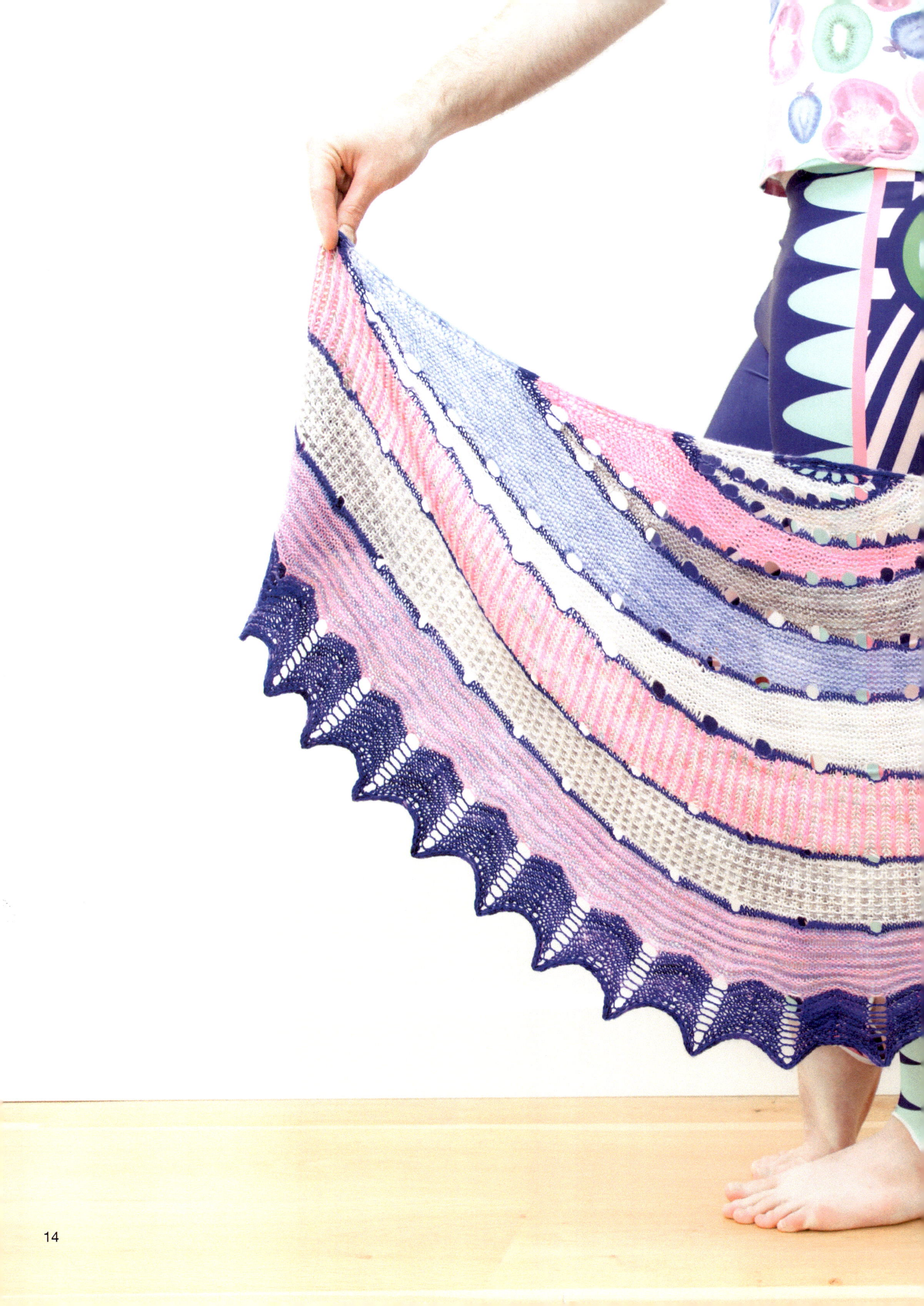

15

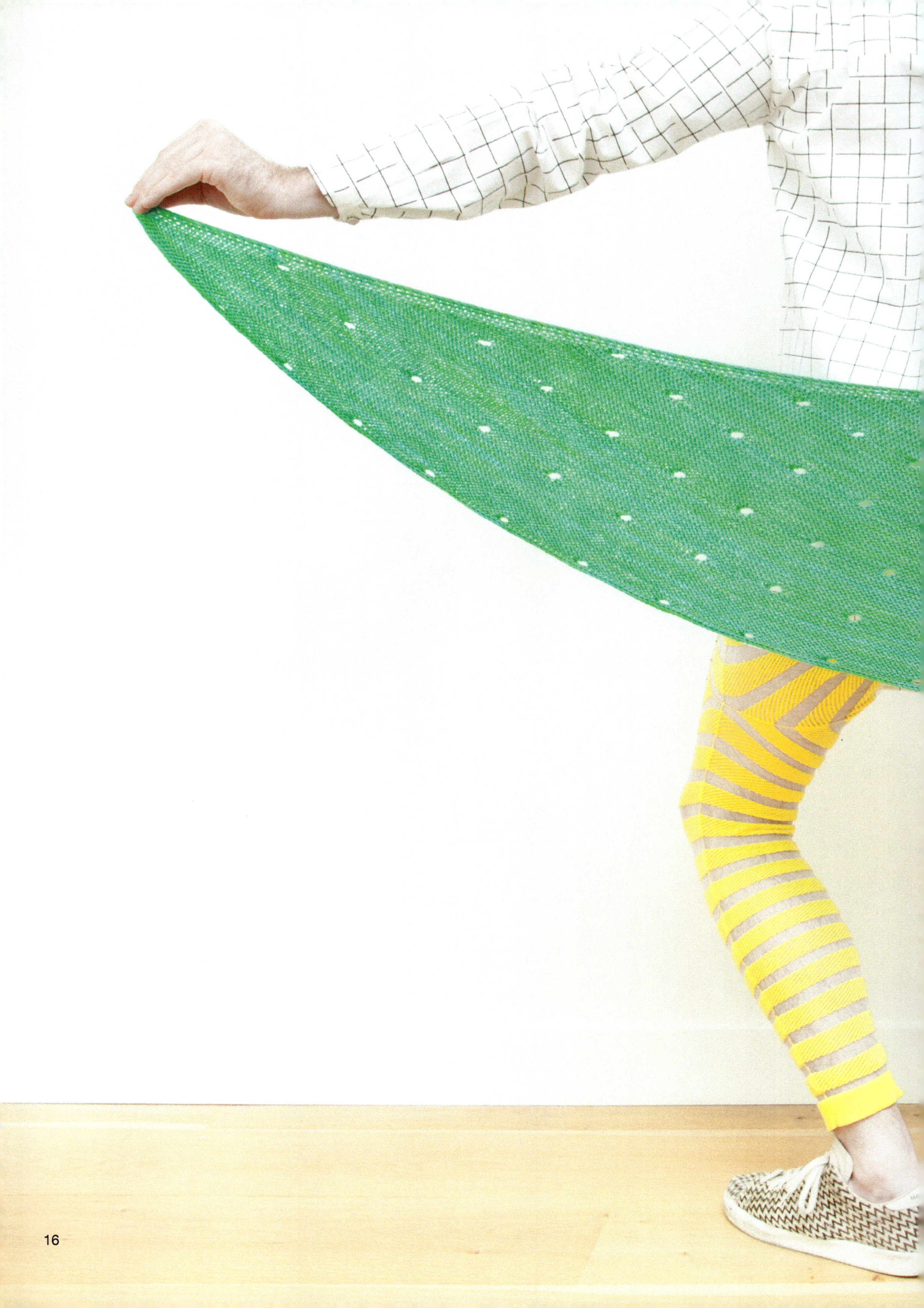

DOTTED RAYS

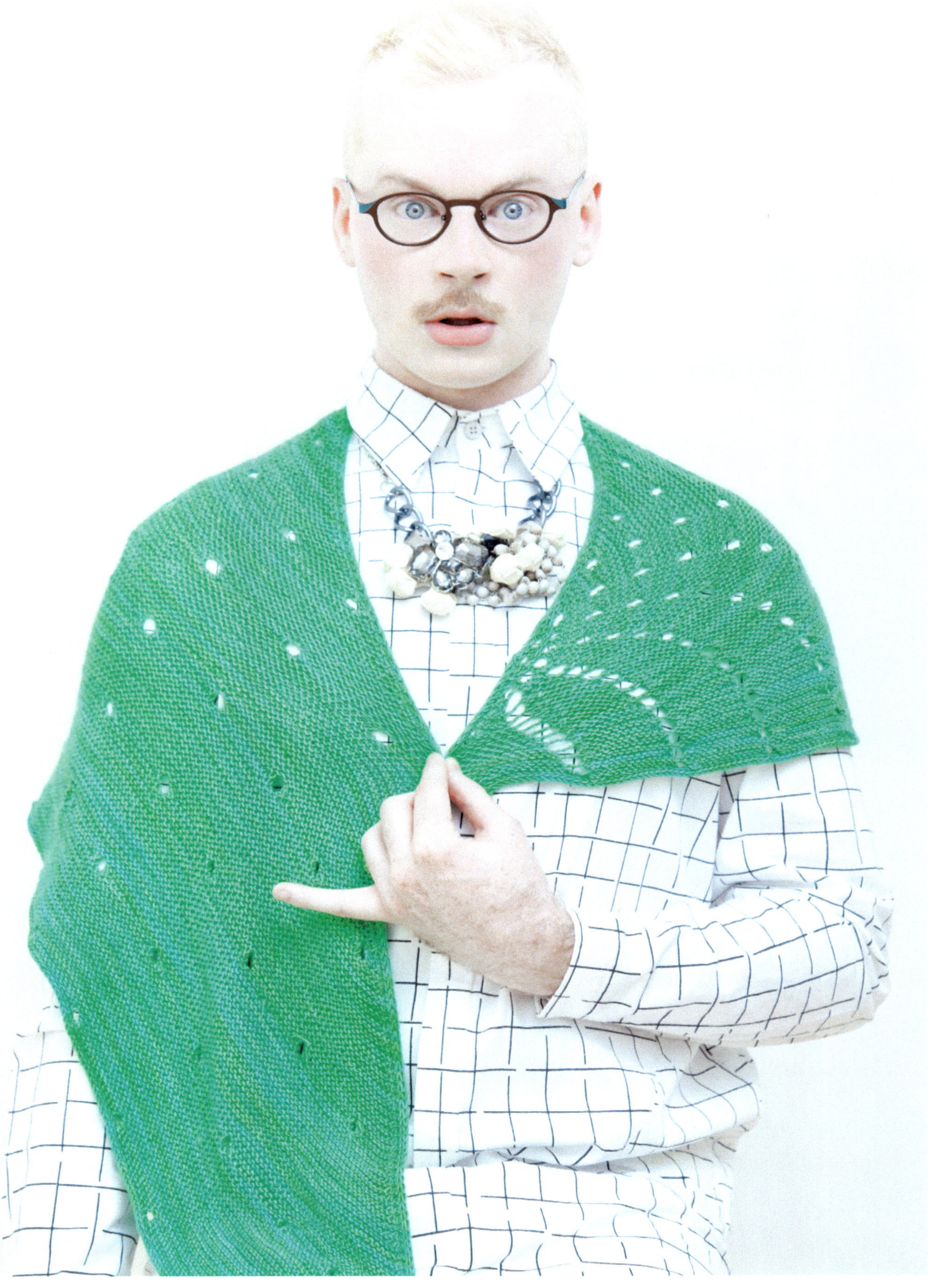

DOTTED RAYS

This arched shawl begins at the center with three stitches while yarn over increases expand the shape. Westknits shortcut rows add length to one side forming rays that gradually increase in size. The repetitive garter stitch and rhythmic sections are easy to knit while still keeping your interest, a perfect travel project! Built in I-cord edges and an I-cord bind off outline the entire shape for a clean finish. Choose one yarn or knit a striped version using your yarn collection.

Size: Small [Large]

Finished Measurements: 60 [92]" / 152 [234] cm wingspan, 13 [22]" / 33 [56]cm longest part between I-cord edges. Measurements taken after blocking.

Yarn: Fingering weight

Shown in: Small Version (green)
The Plucky Knitter Primo Fingering (75% Merino, 20% Cashmere, 5% Nylon; 390yds / 357m per 100g skein), colorway - PH

Large Striped Version (speckles)
Hedgehog Fibres Skinny Singles, Madelinetosh Tosh Merino Light, and various other single ply merino yarns

Yardage: 720 [1200]yds / 658 [1097]m

The large striped version used about 1200yds / 1097m total. Gather a colorful array of scraps and single skeins to work a similarly striped shawl. The last short row wedge of the large size uses about 290yds / 265m and the second to last short row wedge used about 250yds / 229m.

Needles: 47" US 5 / 3.75mm circular

Notions: Tapestry needle

Gauge: 20 sts & 48 rows = 4" / 10cm in garter stitch with US 6 / 4mm needles & fingering weight yarn

Pattern Notes: For a striped shawl, change colors whenever you like. Change colors at the beginning of any RS row. If you want to have a striped look like the large striped version, then add an accent stripe for the yarn over RS and WS rows like Rows 7 & 8, Rows 9 & 10, Rows 11 & 12, etc… These accent stripes feature a contrasting color for only 2 rows (or 1 garter ridge). Then, knit the entire short row wedge in another color. For strong graphic contrast, select yarn over accent stripes (the single garter ridge stripes) that are much brighter or darker than the short row wedge colors.

The pattern is written in a Small and Large Size, but feel free to bind off after any yarn over WS row when the shawl reaches your desired size.

INSTRUCTIONS
SECTION 1

CO 3 sts, *slip 3 sts to left needle, k3, repeat from * 3 more times. You should now have an I-cord 4 rows long. Do not slip sts to left needle after knitting the last 3 sts. Pick up and k3 sts along the edge of I-cord (1 stitch for every row).

Next Row (WS): Pick up and k3 sts from the CO edge, k3, sl3 wyif. 9 sts.

Row 1 (RS): K4, (yo twice, k1) twice, sl3 wyif.
Row 2 (WS): K4, (k1/p1 into double yo, k1) twice, sl3 wyif. 13 sts.

Row 3 (RS): K10, sl3 wyif.
Row 4 (WS): K10, sl3 wyif.

Repeat last 2 rows once more. If you are knitting a striped version with thin accent stripes, introduce your first thin stripe for Rows 7 & 8 and then break your contrast color after Row 8. The thin 2-row accent stripe is always done in the numbered yarn over rows. For example, Rows 9 & 10, 11 & 12, 13 & 14, etc...

Row 7 (RS): K4, (yo twice, k1) 6 times, sl3 wyif.
Row 8 (WS): K4 (k1/p1 in to double yo, k1) 6 times, sl3 wyif. 25 sts.

Next Row (RS): K3, kfb, k15, turn to work WS.
Next Row (WS): K to last 3 sts, sl3 wyif.

Next Row (RS): K3, kfb, k to 4 sts before last turn, turn to work WS.
Next Row (WS): K to last 3 sts, sl3 wyif.

Repeat last 2 rows 3 more times.

Next Row (RS): K4, turn to work WS.
Next Row (WS): K1, sl3 wyif. 30 sts.

Row 9 (RS): K4, (yo twice, k2, ssk) 5 times, yo twice, k3, sl3 wyif.
Row 10 (WS): K6, (k1/p1 into double yo, k3) 5 times, k1/p1 into double yo, k1, sl3 wyif. 37 sts.

Next Row (RS): K3, kfb, k to last 7 sts, turn to work WS.
Next Row (WS): K to last 3 sts, sl3 wyif.

Next Row (RS): K3, kfb, k to 5 sts before last turn, turn to work WS.
Next Row (WS): K to last 3 sts, sl3 wyif.

Repeat last 2 rows 5 more times. 44 sts.

Row 11 (RS): K3, kfb, k1, (ssk, yo twice, k3) 7 times, k1, sl3 wyif.
Row 12 (WS): K7, (k1/p1 into double yo, k4) 7 times, sl3 wyif. 52 sts.

Next Row (RS): K3, kfb, k to last 8 sts, turn to work WS.
Next Row (WS): K to last 3 sts, sl3 wyif.

Next Row (RS): K3, kfb, k to 6 sts before last turn, turn to work WS.
Next Row (WS): K to last 3 sts, sl3 wyif.

Repeat last 2 rows 6 more times. 60 sts.

Next Row (RS): K4, turn to work WS.
Next Row (WS): K1, sl3 wyif.

Row 13 (RS): K4, (yo twice, k4, ssk) 8 times, yo twice, k5, sl3 wyif.
Row 14 (WS): K8, (k1/p1 into double yo, k5) 8 times, k1/p1 into double yo, k1, sl3 wyif. 70 sts.

Next Row (RS): K3, kfb, k to last 9 sts, turn to work WS.
Next Row (WS): K to last 3 sts, sl3 wyif.

Next Row (RS): K3, kfb, k to 7 sts before last turn, turn to work WS.
Next Row (WS): K to last 3 sts, sl3 wyif.

Repeat last 2 rows 8 more times. 80 sts.

Row 15 (RS): K3, kfb, k2 (ssk, yo twice, k5) 10 times, k1, sl3 wyif.

Row 16 (WS): K9, (k1/p1 into double yo, k6) 9 times, k1/p1 into double yo, k5, sl3 wyif. 91 sts.

Next Row (RS): K3, kfb, k to last 10 sts, turn to work WS.
Next Row (WS): K to last 3 sts, sl3 wyif.

Next Row (RS): K3, kfb, k to 8 sts before last turn, turn to work WS.
Next Row (WS): K to last 3 sts, sl3 wyif.

Repeat last 2 rows 9 more times. 102 sts.

Next Row (RS): K4, turn to work WS.
Next Row (WS): K1, sl3 wyif.

Row 17 (RS): K3, kfb, (yo twice, k6, ssk) 11 times, yo twice, k7, sl3 wyif.
Row 18 (WS): K10, (k1/p1 into double yo, k7) 11 times, k1/p1 into double yo, k2, sl3 wyif. 116 sts.

Next Row (RS): K3, kfb, k to last 11 sts, turn to work WS.
Next Row (WS): K to last 3 sts, sl3 wyif.

Next Row (RS): K3, kfb, k to 9 sts before last turn, turn to work WS.
Next Row (WS): K to last 3 sts, sl3 wyif.

Repeat last 2 rows 11 more times. 129 sts.

Row 19 (RS): K3, kfb, k4, (ssk, yo twice, k7) 13 times, k1, sl3 wyif.
Row 20 (WS): K11, (k1/p1 into double yo, k8) 12 times, k1/p1 into double yo, k7, sl3 wyif. 143 sts.

Next Row (RS): K3, kfb, k to last 12 sts, turn to work WS.
Next Row (WS): K to last 3 sts, sl3 wyif.

Next Row (RS): K3, kfb, k to 10 sts before last turn, turn to work WS.
Next Row (WS): K to last 3 sts, sl3 wyif.

Repeat last 2 rows 13 more times. 158 sts.

Row 21 (RS): K3, kfb, (ssk, yo twice, k8) 15 times, k1, sl3 wyif.
Row 22 (WS): K12, (k1/p1 into double yo, k9) 14 times, k1/p1 into double yo, k3, sl3 wyif. 174 sts.

Next Row (RS): K3, kfb, k to last 13 sts, turn to work WS.
Next Row (WS): K to last 3 sts, sl3 wyif.

Next Row (RS): K3, kfb, k to 11 sts before last turn, turn to work WS.
Next Row (WS): K to last 3 sts, sl3 wyif.

Repeat last 2 rows 14 more times. 190 sts.

Row 23 (RS): K3, kfb, k6, (ssk, yo twice, k9) 16 times, k1, sl3 wyif.
Row 24 (WS): K13, (k1/p1 into double yo, k10) 15 times, k1/p1 into double yo, k9, sl3 wyif. 207 sts.

Next Row (RS): K3, kfb, k to last 14 sts, turn to work WS.
Next Row (WS): K to last 3 sts, sl3 wyif.

Next Row (RS): K3, kfb, k to 12 sts before last turn, turn to work WS.
Next Row (WS): K to last 3 sts, sl3 wyif.

Repeat last 2 rows 16 more times. 225 sts.

Row 25 (RS): K3, kfb, k1, (ssk, yo twice, k10) 18 times, k1, sl3 wyif.
Row 26 (WS): K14, (k1/p1 into double yo, k11) 17 times, k1/p1 into double yo, k4, sl3 wyif. 244 sts.

Next Row (RS): K3, kfb, k to last 15 sts, turn to work WS.
Next Row (WS): K to last 3 sts, sl3 wyif.

Next Row (RS): K3, kfb, k to 13 sts before last turn, turn to work WS.
Next Row (WS): K to last 3 sts, sl3 wyif.

Repeat last 2 rows 17 more times. 263 sts.

Small Size
1 color

Row 27 (RS): K3, kfb, k8, (ssk, yo twice, k11) 19 times, k1, sl3 wyif.
Row 28 (WS): K15, (k1/p1 into double yo, k12) 18 times, k1/p1 into double yo, k11, sl3 wyif. 283 sts.

Next Row (RS): K3, kfb, k to last 16 sts, turn to work WS.
Next Row (WS): K to last 3 sts, sl3 wyif.

Next Row (RS): K3, kfb, k to 14 sts before last turn, turn to work WS.
Next Row (WS): K to last 3 sts, sl3 wyif.

Repeat last 2 rows 19 more times. 304 sts.

Row 29 (RS): K3, kfb, k2, (ssk, yo twice, k12) 21 times, k1, sl3 wyif.
Row 30 (WS): K16, (k1/p1 into double yo, k13) 20 times, k1/p1 into double yo, k6, sl3 wyif. 327 sts.

Next Row (RS): K3, kfb, k to last 17 sts, turn to work WS.
Next Row (WS): K to last 3 sts, sl3 wyif.

Next Row (RS): K3, kfb, k to 15 sts before last turn, turn to work WS.
Next Row (WS): K to last 3 sts, sl3 wyif.

Repeat last 2 rows 20 more times. 349 sts.

Row 31 (RS): K3, kfb, k10, (ssk, yo twice, k13) 22 times, k1, sl3 wyif.
Row 32 (WS): K17, (k1/p1 into double yo, k14) 21 times, k1/p1 into double yo, k12, sl3 wyif. 371 sts.

Small Size Only
Skip to FINISHING instructions.

Large Size Only
Next Row (RS): K3, kfb, k to last 18 sts, turn to work WS.
Next Row (WS): K to last 3 sts, sl3 wyif.

Next Row (RS): K3, kfb, k to 16 sts before last turn, turn to work WS.
Next Row (WS): K to last 3 sts, sl3 wyif.

Repeat last 2 rows 22 more times. 395 sts.

Row 33 (RS): K3, kfb, k3, (ssk, yo twice, k14) 24 times, k1, sl3 wyif.
Row 34 (WS): K18, (k1/p1 into double yo, k15) 23 times, k1/p1 into double yo, k6, sl3 wyif. 420 sts.

Next Row (RS): K3, kfb, k to last 19 sts, turn to work WS.
Next Row (WS): K to last 3 sts, sl3 wyif.

Next Row (RS): K3, kfb, k to 17 sts before last turn, turn to work WS.
Next Row (WS): K to last 3 sts, sl3 wyif.

Repeat last 2 rows 23 more times. 445 sts.

Row 35 (RS): K3, kfb, k12, (ssk, yo twice, k15) 25 times, k1, sl3 wyif.
Row 36 (WS): K19, (k1/p1 into double yo, k16) 24 times, k1/p1 into double yo, k14, sl3 wyif. 471 sts.

Next Row (RS): K3, kfb, k to last 20 sts, turn to work WS.
Next Row (WS): K to last 3 sts, sl3 wyif.

Next Row (RS): K3, kfb, k to 18 sts before last turn, turn to work WS.
Next Row (WS): K to last 3 sts, sl3 wyif.

Repeat last 2 rows 25 more times. 498 sts.

Row 37 (RS): K3, kfb, k4, (ssk, yo twice, k16) 27 times, k1, sl3 wyif.
Row 38 (WS): K20, (k1/p1 into double yo, k17) 26 times, k1/p1 into double yo, k7, sl3 wyif. 526 sts.

FINISHING

BO all sts on the next RS row using an I-cord BO as follows, *K2, k2tog tbl, slip 3 sts back onto left needle, repeat from * to last 3 sts. 6 total sts remain. Graft the 6 remaining sts together. Weave in ends and block finished shawl.

Large Size
La Bien Aimée
Merino Singles

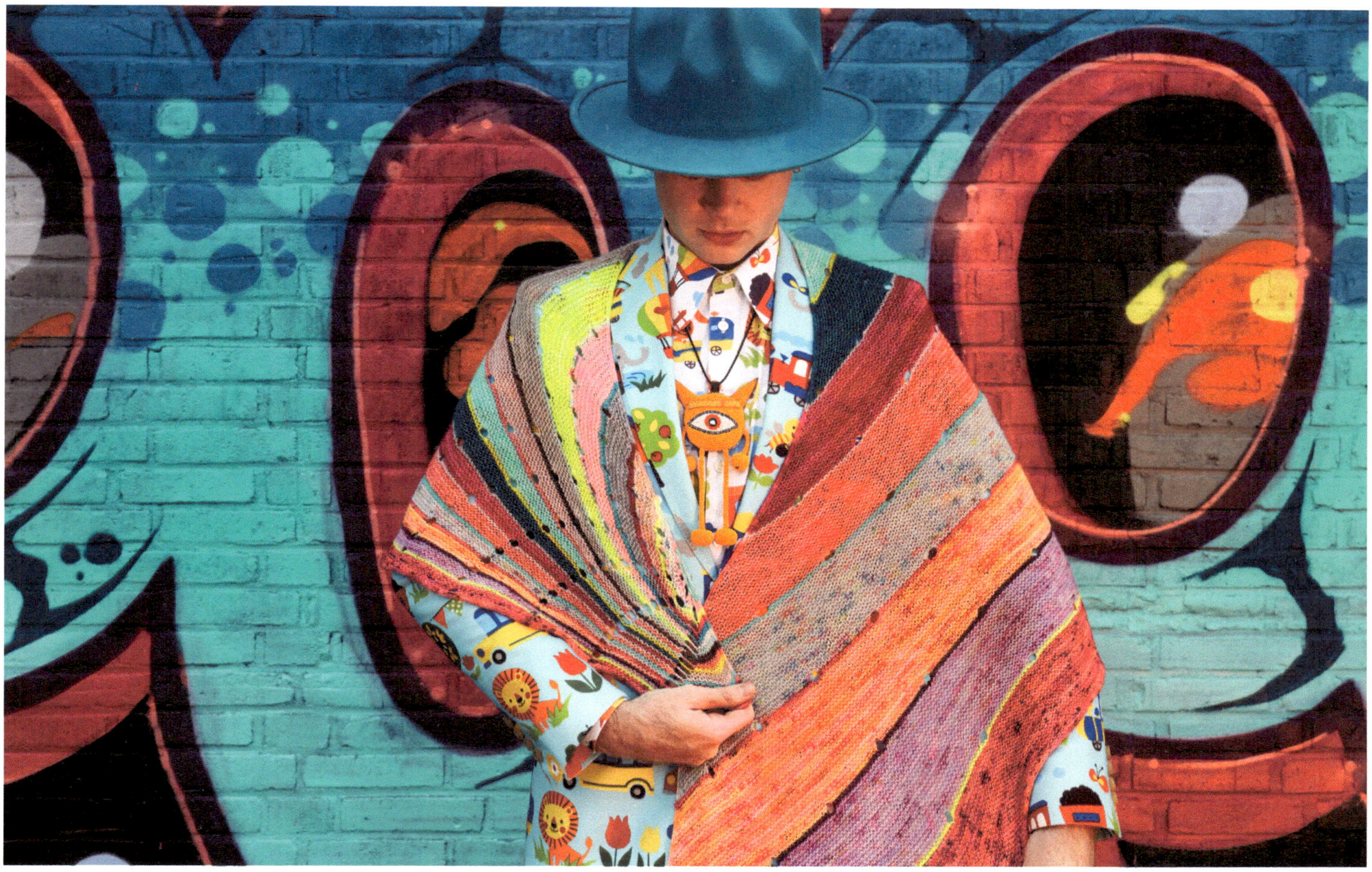

26

Large Size
Hedgehog Fibres Skinny Singles
La Bien Aimée Merino Singles
Qing Fiber Merino Single Ply

Large Size
Das Mondschaf
Sockenwolle Merino

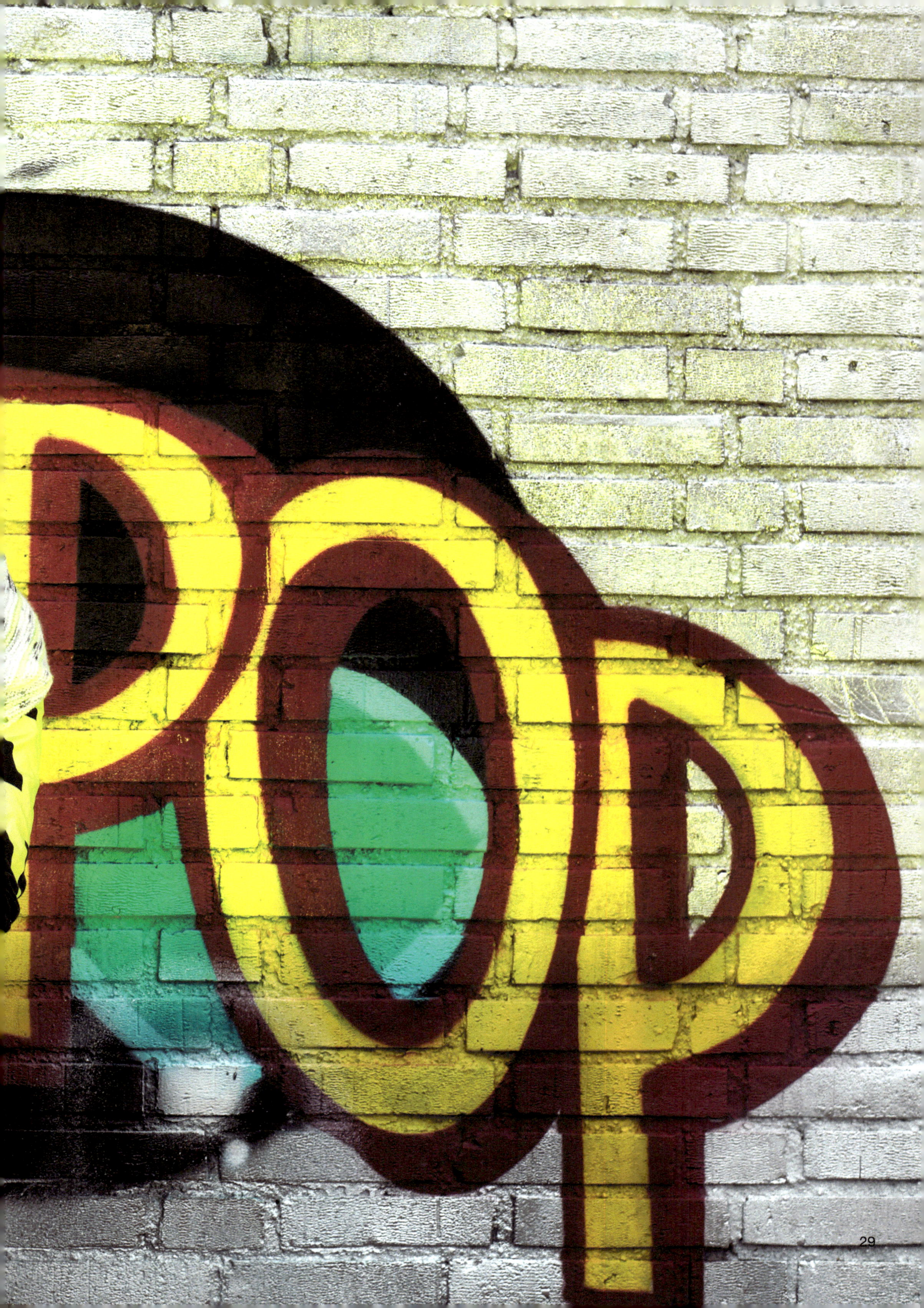
POP

30

THE DOODLER

THE DOODLER

Choose three colors to knit this playful shawl. Begin with Westknits shortcut rows and increase to built the striped section. Continue with a contrasting color to knit a large cable that grows across the edge. Pick up stitches in a third color to knit the wavy border. Choose between a simple I-cord bind off or add decorative picot clusters for an embellished edge.

Finished Measurements: 60" / 152cm wingspan length, 24" / 61cm from cable edging to wavy bind off edge. Measurements taken after blocking.

Yarn: Fingering weight

Shown in: Pink/Yellow Version
Hedgehog Fibres Skinny Singles (100% Merino Wool;
Color A - Seed
Color B - Pollen
Color C - Tulp

Purple Version
Hedgehog Fibres Skinny Singles
Color A - Urchin
Color B - Birthday Cake
Color C - Purple Reign

Yardage: Color A - 355yds / 325m
Color B - 285yds / 261m
Color C - 395yds / 361m

Needles: 40" US 4 / 3.5mm circular

Notions: Cable needle or DPN, 8 stitch markers, tapestry needle

Gauge: 22 sts & 52 rows = 4" / 10cm in garter stitch

Abbreviations:
C16B: (cable 16 back) slip 8 stitches onto cable needle or DPN and hold in back of work, knit 8, knit 8 stitches from cable needle or DPN. Stitches increase throughout Section 2, so the cables will increase to C18B, C20B, C22B, etc... Always place the first half of the stitches onto cable needle or DPN and hold them in back. For example, C24B: slip 12 stitches onto cable needle or DPN and hold in back of work, knit 12 stitches, knit 12 stitches from cable needle or DPN.

33

INSTRUCTIONS
SECTION 1

Using color A, CO 3 sts using the long tail CO, *slip 3 sts to left needle, k3, repeat from * 25 more times. Pick up and k25 sts along I-cord edge, turn to work WS. 28 sts.

Next Row (WS): Pick up and k3 sts from CO edge, k25, sl3 wyif. 31 sts.

Wedge 1
Row 1 (RS): K3, kfb, k to last 3 sts, turn to work WS.
Row 2 (WS): K to last 3 sts, sl3 wyif.

Row 3 (RS): K3, kfb, k to 5 sts before last turn, turn to work WS.
Row 4 (WS): K to last 3 sts, sl3 wyif.

Repeat last 2 rows 4 more times. 37 sts.

Next Row (RS): K3. Using color B, kfb, (k3, k2tog, yo) 6 times, sl3 wyif. 38 sts.
Next Row (WS): K to last 3 sts, sl3 wyif. Break color B.

Wedge 2
Row 1 (RS): Using color A, k to last 4 sts, turn to work WS.
Row 2 (WS): K to last 3 sts, sl3 wyif.

Row 3 (RS): K to 5 sts before last turn, turn to work WS.
Row 4 (WS): K to last 3 sts, sl3 wyif.

Repeat last 2 rows 4 more times.

Next Row (RS): K3. Using color B, k1, (k3, k2tog, yo) 6 times, k1, sl3 wyif.
Next Row (WS): K to last 3 sts, sl3 wyif. Break color B.

Wedge 3
Row 1 (RS): Using color A, k3, kfb, k to last 5 sts, turn to work WS.
Row 2 (WS): K to last 3 sts, sl3 wyif.

Row 3 (RS): K3, kfb, k to 5 sts before last turn, turn to work WS.
Row 4 (WS): K to last 3 sts, sl3 wyif.

Repeat last 2 rows 5 more times. 45 sts.

Next Row (RS): K3. Using color B, kfb, k1, (k3, k2tog, yo) 7 times, k2, sl3 wyif. 46 sts.
Next Row (WS): K to last 3 sts, sl3 wyif. Break color B.

Wedge 4
Row 1 (RS): Using color A, k to last 6 sts, turn to work WS.
Row 2 (WS): K to last 3 sts, sl3 wyif.

Row 3 (RS): K to 5 sts before last turn, turn to work WS.
Row 4 (WS): K to last 3 sts, sl3 wyif.

Repeat last 2 rows 5 more times.

Next Row (RS): K3. Using color B, k2, (k3, k2tog, yo) 7 times, k3, sl3 wyif.
Next Row (WS): K to last 3 sts, sl3 wyif. Break color B.

Wedge 5
Row 1 (RS): Using color A, k3, kfb, k to last 7 sts, turn to work WS.
Row 2 (WS): K to last 3 sts, sl3 wyif.

Row 3 (RS): K3, kfb, k to 5 sts before last turn, turn to work WS.
Row 4 (WS): K to last 3 sts, sl3 wyif.

Repeat last 2 rows 7 more times. 55 sts.

Next Row (RS): K3. Using color B, kfb, k2, k2tog, yo, (k3, k2tog, yo) 8 times, k4, sl3 wyif. 56 sts.
Next Row (WS): K to last 3 sts, sl3 wyif. Break color B.

Wedge 6
Row 1 (RS): Using color A, k to last 8 sts, turn to work WS.
Row 2 (WS): K to last 3 sts, sl3 wyif.

Row 3 (RS): K to 5 sts before last turn, turn to work WS.
Row 4 (WS): K to last 3 sts, sl3 wyif.

Repeat last 2 rows 7 more times.

Next Row (RS): K3. Using color B, (k3, k2tog, yo) 9 times, k5, sl3 wyif.
Next Row (WS): K to last 3 sts, sl3 wyif. Break color B.

Wedge 7
Row 1 (RS): Using color A, k3, kfb, k to last 9 sts, turn to work WS.
Row 2 (WS): K to last 3 sts, sl3 wyif.

Row 3 (RS): K3, kfb, k to 5 sts before last turn, turn to work WS.
Row 4 (WS): K to last 3 sts, sl3 wyif.

Repeat last 2 rows 9 more times. 67 sts.

Next Row (RS): K3. Using color B, kfb, k2, k2tog, yo, (k3, k2tog, yo) 10 times, k6, sl3 wyif. 68 sts.
Next Row (WS): K to last 3 sts, sl3 wyif. Break color B.

Wedge 8
Row 1 (RS): Using color A, k to last 10 sts, turn to work WS.
Row 2 (WS): K to last 3 sts, sl3 wyif.

Row 3 (RS): K to 5 sts before last turn, turn to work WS.
Row 4 (WS): K to last 3 sts, sl3 wyif.

Repeat last 2 rows 9 more times.

Next Row (RS): K3. Using color B, (k3, k2tog, yo) 11 times, k7, sl3 wyif.
Next Row (WS): K to last 3 sts, sl3 wyif. Break color B.

Wedge 9
Row 1 (RS): Using color A, k3, kfb, k to last 11 sts, turn to work WS.
Row 2 (WS): K to last 3 sts, sl3 wyif.

Row 3 (RS): K3, kfb, k to 5 sts before last turn, turn to work WS.
Row 4 (WS): K to last 3 sts, sl3 wyif.

Repeat last 2 rows 11 more times. 81 sts.

Next Row (RS): K3. Using color B, kfb, k1, (k3, k2tog, yo) 13 times, k8, sl3 wyif. 82 sts.
Next Row (WS): K to last 3 sts, sl3 wyif. Break color B.

Wedge 10
Row 1 (RS): Using color A, k to last 12 sts, turn to work WS.
Row 2 (WS): K to last 3 sts, sl3 wyif.

Row 3 (RS): K to 5 sts before last turn, turn to work WS.
Row 4 (WS): K to last 3 sts, sl3 wyif.

Repeat last 2 rows 11 more times.

Next Row (RS): K3. Using color B, k2, (k3, k2tog, yo) 13 times, k9, sl3 wyif.
Next Row (WS): K to last 3 sts, sl3 wyif. Break color B.

Wedge 11
Row 1 (RS): Using color A, k3, kfb, k to last 13 sts, turn to work WS.
Row 2 (WS): K to last 3 sts, sl3 wyif.

Row 3 (RS): K3, kfb, k to 5 sts before last turn, turn to work WS.
Row 4 (WS): K to last 3 sts, sl3 wyif.

Repeat last 2 rows 14 more times. 98 sts.

Next Row (RS): K3. Using color B, kfb, k1, (k3, k2tog, yo) 16 times, k10, sl3 wyif. 99 sts.
Next Row (WS): K to last 3 sts, sl3 wyif. Break color B.

Wedge 12
Row 1 (RS): Using color A, k to last 14 sts, turn to work WS.
Row 2 (WS): K to last 3 sts, sl3 wyif.

Row 3 (RS): K to 5 sts before last turn, turn to work WS.
Row 4 (WS): K to last 3 sts, sl3 wyif.

Repeat last 2 rows 14 more times.

Next Row (RS): K3. Using color B, k2, (k3, k2tog, yo) 16 times, k11, sl3 wyif.
Next Row (WS): K to last 3 sts, sl3 wyif. Break color B.

Wedge 13
Row 1 (RS): Using color A, k3, kfb, k to last 15 sts, turn to work WS.
Row 2 (WS): K to last 3 sts, sl3 wyif.

Row 3 (RS): K3, kfb, k to 5 sts before last turn, turn to work WS.
Row 4 (WS): K to last 3 sts, sl3 wyif.

Repeat last 2 rows 18 more times. 119 sts.

Next Row (RS): K3. Using color B, kfb, (k3, k2tog, yo) 20 times, k12, sl3 wyif. 120 sts.
Next Row (WS): K to last 3 sts, sl3 wyif. Break color B.

Wedge 14
Row 1 (RS): Using color A, k to last 16 sts, turn to work WS.
Row 2 (WS): K to last 3 sts, sl3 wyif.

Row 3 (RS): K to 5 sts before last turn, turn to work WS.
Row 4 (WS): K to last 3 sts, sl3 wyif.

Repeat last 2 rows 18 more times.

Next Row (RS): K3. Using color B, k1, (k3, k2tog, yo) 20 times, k13, sl3 wyif.
Next Row (WS): K to last 3 sts, sl3 wyif. Break color B.

Wedge 15
Row 1 (RS): Using color A, k3, kfb, k to last 17 sts, turn to work WS.
Row 2 (WS): K to last 3 sts, sl3 wyif.

Row 3 (RS): K3, kfb, k to 5 sts before last turn, turn to work WS.
Row 4 (WS): K to last 3 sts, sl3 wyif.

Repeat last 2 rows 23 more times. 145 sts.

Next Row (RS): K3. Using color B, kfb, k2, k2tog, yo, (k3, k2tog, yo) 24 times, k14, sl3 wyif. 146 sts.
Next Row (WS): K to last 3 sts, sl3 wyif. Break color B.

Wedge 16
Row 1 (RS): Using color A, k to last 18 sts, turn to work WS.
Row 2 (WS): K to last 3 sts, sl3 wyif.

Row 3 (RS): K to 5 sts before last turn, turn to work WS.
Row 4 (WS): K to last 3 sts, sl3 wyif.

Repeat last 2 rows 23 more times.

Next Row (RS): K3. Using color B, (k3, k2tog, yo) 25 times, k15, sl3 wyif.
Next Row (WS): K to last 3 sts, sl3 wyif. Break color B.

Wedge 17
Row 1 (RS): Using color A, k3, kfb, k to last 19 sts, turn to work WS.
Row 2 (WS): K to last 3 sts, sl3 wyif.

37

Row 3 (RS): K3, kfb, k to 5 sts before last turn, turn to work WS.
Row 4 (WS): K to last 3 sts, sl3 wyif.

Repeat last 2 rows 29 more times. 177 sts.

SECTION 2
Next Row (RS): K3. Break color A. Using color B, kfb, k2, k2tog, yo, (k3, k2tog, yo) 30 times, k16, sl3 wyif. 178 sts.
Next Row (WS): K19, ssk, turn to work RS.

Cable 1
Row 1 (RS): Sl1 wyif, place yarn in back, C16B, sl3 wyif.
Row 2 (WS): K19, ssk, turn to work RS.

Row 3 (RS): Sl1 wyif, place yarn in back, k16, sl3 wyif.
Row 4 (WS): K19, ssk, turn to work RS.

Repeat last 2 rows 8 more times.

Row 21 (RS): Sl1 wyif, place yarn in back, (kfb, k7) twice, sl3 wyif. 22 sts.
Row 22 (WS): K21, ssk, turn to work RS.

Cable 2
Row 1 (RS): Sl1 wyif, place yarn in back, C18B, sl3 wyif.
Row 2 (WS): K21, ssk, turn to work RS.

Row 3 (RS): Sl1 wyif, place yarn in back, k18, sl3 wyif.
Row 4 (WS): K21, ssk, turn to work RS.

Repeat last 2 rows 9 more times.

Row 23 (RS): Sl1 wyif, place yarn in back, (kfb, k8) twice, sl3 wyif. 24 sts.
Row 24 (WS): K23, ssk, turn to work RS.

Cable 3
Row 1 (RS): Sl1 wyif, place yarn in back, C20B, sl3 wyif.
Row 2 (WS): K23, ssk, turn to work RS.

Row 3 (RS): Sl1 wyif, place yarn in back, k20, sl3 wyif.
Row 4 (WS): K23, ssk, turn to work RS.

Repeat last 2 rows 10 more times.

Row 25 (RS): Sl1 wyif, place yarn in back, (kfb, k9) twice, sl3 wyif. 26 sts.
Row 26 (WS): K25, ssk, turn to work RS.

Cable 4
Row 1 (RS): Sl1 wyif, place yarn in back, C22B, sl3 wyif.
Row 2 (WS): K25, ssk, turn to work RS.

Row 3 (RS): Sl1 wyif, place yarn in back, k22, sl3 wyif.
Row 4 (WS): K25, ssk, turn to work RS.

Repeat last 2 rows 11 more times.

Row 27 (RS): Sl1 wyif, place yarn in back, (kfb, k10) twice, sl3 wyif. 28 sts.
Row 28 (WS): K27, ssk, turn to work RS.

Cable 5
Row 1 (RS): Sl1 wyif, place yarn in back, C24B, sl3 wyif.
Row 2 (WS): K27, ssk, turn to work RS.

Row 3 (RS): Sl1 wyif, place yarn in back, k24, sl3 wyif.
Row 4 (WS): K27, ssk, turn to work RS.

Repeat last 2 rows 12 more times.

Row 29 (RS): Sl1 wyif, place yarn in back, (kfb, k11) twice, sl3 wyif. 30 sts.
Row 30 (WS): K29, ssk, turn to work RS.

Cable 6
Row 1 (RS): Sl1 wyif, place yarn in back, C26B, sl3 wyif.
Row 2 (WS): K29, ssk, turn to work RS.

Row 3 (RS): Sl1 wyif, place yarn in back, k26, sl3 wyif.
Row 4 (WS): K29, ssk, turn to work RS.

Repeat last 2 rows 13 more times.

Row 31 (RS): Sl1 wyif, place yarn in back, (kfb, k12) twice, sl3 wyif. 32 sts.
Row 32 (WS): K31, ssk, turn to work RS.

Cable 7
Row 1 (RS): Sl1 wyif, place yarn in back, C28B, sl3 wyif.
Row 2 (WS): K31, ssk, turn to work RS.

Row 3 (RS): Sl1 wyif, place yarn in back, k28, sl3 wyif.
Row 4 (WS): K31, ssk, turn to work RS.

Repeat last 2 rows 14 more times.

Row 33 (RS): Sl1 wyif, place yarn in back, (kfb, k13) twice, sl3 wyif. 34 sts.
Row 34 (WS): K33, ssk, turn to work RS.

Cable 8
Row 1 (RS): Sl1 wyif, place yarn in back, C30B, sl3 wyif.
Row 2 (WS): K33, ssk, turn to work RS.

Row 3 (RS): Sl1 wyif, place yarn in back, k30, sl3 wyif.
Row 4 (WS): K33, ssk, turn to work RS.

Repeat last 2 rows 15 more times.

Row 35 (RS): Sl1 wyif, place yarn in back, (kfb, k14) twice, sl3 wyif. 36 sts.
Row 36 (WS): K35, ssk, turn to work RS.

Cable 9
Row 1 (RS): Sl1 wyif, place yarn in back, C32B, sl3 wyif.
Row 2 (WS): K35, ssk, turn to work RS.

Row 3 (RS): Sl1 wyif, place yarn in back, k32, sl3 wyif.
Row 4 (WS): K35, ssk, turn to work RS.

Repeat last 2 rows 16 more times.

Row 37 (RS): Sl1 wyif, place yarn in back, (kfb, k15) twice, sl3 wyif. 38 sts.
Row 38 (WS): K37, ssk, turn to work RS.

Cable 10
Row 1 (RS): Sl1 wyif, place yarn in back, C34B, sl3 wyif.
Row 2 (WS): K37, ssk, turn to work RS.

Row 3 (RS): Sl1 wyif, place yarn in back, k34, sl3 wyif.
Row 4 (WS): K37, ssk, turn to work RS.

Repeat last 2 rows 17 more times.

Row 39 (RS): Sl1 wyif, place yarn in back, k to last 3 sts, sl3 wyif.
Row 40 (WS): BO all sts as follows, *k2, k2tog tbl, slip 3 sts to left needle, repeat from * to last 3 sts. 6 total sts remain. Graft remaining sts together.

SECTION 3

This section has 2 size options: Wedges 1-3 for the regular size or add an additional Wedge 4 for the expanded size.
The color C yardage estimate is for the expanded size (Wedges 1-4) using Hedgehog Fibres Skinny Singles (a single ply merino wool) with a gauge of 22 sts & 52 rows = 4" / 10cm in garter stitch.
If you ran out of color A in SECTION 1 or used more than the recommended yardage, then only work the instructions through Wedge 3.

Wedges 1-3 should use considerably less yarn than the recommended color C amount of 395yds / 361m.
If you matched the yardage estimates in the previous sections, then work the extra Wedge 4.
Color C uses more yarn than color A so it's still possible you may run out of color C in Wedge 4 if you used more than 355yds / 325m of color A in SECTION 1.
SECTION 3 uses color C the entire time, but feel free to substitute an additional color pop to any Wedge if want to add more color!
If you have any doubt about how many wedges to knit, then only knit Wedges 1-3 to be safe.

Using color C and with RS facing, pick up and k3 sts from the corner of the I-cord CO from SECTION 1.

Pick up and k263 sts along the jagged color A I-cord edge from SECTION 1. (Pick up into each I-cord stitch that rolls towards the WS.) Continue to pick up and k34 sts from the color B I-cord BO. Turn to work WS. 300 sts.

41

Next Row (WS): Pick up and k3 I-cord sts from the corner of color B. Continue working the WS row with the instructions below.
K22, (yo, k1) 25 times, k7, k2tog 6 times, pm, k2tog 5 times.
K4, (yo, k1) 23 times, k6, k2tog 5 times, pm, k2tog 4 times.
K2, (yo, k1) 21 times, k2, k2tog 4 times, pm, k2tog 3 times.
K4, (yo, k1) 17 times, k1, k2tog 3 times, pm, k2tog 2 times.
K4, (yo, k1) 13 times, k1, k2tog 3 times, pm, k2tog twice.
K3, (yo, k1) 11 times, k2, k2tog twice, pm, k2tog.
K4, (yo, k1) 9 times, k1, k2tog twice, pm, k2tog.
K3, (yo, k1) 7 times, k2tog twice, pm, k2tog.
K3, (yo, k1) 5 times, k5, sl3 wyif. 388 sts.

Wedge 1
While you knit your rows, slip the stitch markers onto the right needle when you reach them.
Row 1 (RS): K to last 3 sts, sl3 wyif.
Row 2 (WS): K to last stitch marker, slm, k1, turn to work RS.

Row 3 (RS): K to last 3 sts, sl3 wyif.
Row 4 (WS): K to the stitch marker before the previous short row turn, slm, k1, turn to work RS.

Repeat Rows 3 & 4 6 more times. You will be turning around 1 stitch marker earlier each time.

Row 17 (RS): K to last 3 sts, sl3 wyif.
Row 18 (WS): K37, (yo, k1) 25 times, k8, k2tog 9 times, slm, k2tog 8 times.
K4, (yo, k1) 23 times, k9, k2tog 7 times, slm, k2tog 6 times.
K4, (yo, k1) 21 times, k5, k2tog 6 times, slm, k2tog 5 times.
K5, (yo, k1) 17 times, k5, k2tog 4 times, slm, k2tog 3 times.
K6, (yo, k1) 13 times, k3, k2tog 4 times, slm, k2tog 3 times.
K4, (yo, k1) 11 times, k4, k2tog 3 times, slm, k2tog twice.
K5, (yo, k1) 9 times, k4, k2tog twice, slm, k2tog twice.
K3, (yo, k1) 7 times, k2, k2tog twice, slm, k2tog.
K4, (yo, k1) 5 times, k8, sl3 wyif. 452 sts.

Wedge 2
Row 1 (RS): K to last 3 sts, sl3 wyif.
Row 2 (WS): K to last stitch marker, slm, k1, turn to work RS.

Row 3 (RS): K to last 3 sts, sl3 wyif.
Row 4 (WS): K to the stitch marker before the previous short row turn, slm, k1, turn to work RS.

Repeat Rows 3 & 4 6 more times. You will be turning around 1 stitch marker earlier each time.

Row 17 (RS): K to last 3 sts, sl3 wyif.
Row 18 (WS): K49, (yo, k1) 25 times, k12, k2tog 9 times, slm, k2tog 8 times.
K7, (yo, k1) 23 times, k14, k2tog 7 times, slm, k2tog 6 times.
K8, (yo, k1) 21 times, k10, k2tog 6 times, slm, k2tog 5 times.
K8, (yo, k1) 17 times, k10, k2tog 4 times, slm, k2tog 3 times.
K9, (yo, k1) 13 times, k6, k2tog 4 times, slm, k2tog 3 times.
K6, (yo, k1) 11 times, k7, k2tog 3 times, slm, k2tog twice.
K7, (yo, k1) 9 times, k7, k2tog twice, slm, k2tog twice.
K4, (yo, k1) 7 times, k4, k2tog twice, slm, k2tog.
K5, (yo, k1) 5 times, k11, sl3 wyif. 516 sts.

Wedge 3
Row 1 (RS): K to last 3 sts, sl3 wyif.
Row 2 (WS): K to last stitch marker, slm, k1, turn to work RS.

Row 3 (RS): K to last 3 sts, sl3 wyif.
Row 4 (WS): K to the stitch marker before the previous short row turn, slm, k1, turn to work RS.

Repeat Rows 3 & 4 6 more times. You will be turning around 1 stitch marker earlier each time.

Row 17 (RS): K to last 3 sts, sl3 wyif.
Row 18 (WS): K61, (yo, k1) 25 times, k16, k2tog 9 times, slm, k2tog 8 times.
K10, (yo, k1) 23 times, k19, k2tog 7 times, slm, k2tog 6 times.
K12, (yo, k1) 21 times, k15, k2tog 6 times, slm, k2tog 5 times.
K11, (yo, k1) 17 times, k15, k2tog 4 times, slm, k2tog 3 times.
K12, (yo, k1) 13 times, k9, k2tog 4 times, slm, k2tog 3 times.
K8, (yo, k1) 11 times, k10, k2tog 3 times, slm, k2tog twice.
K9, (yo, k1) 9 times, k10, k2tog twice, slm, k2tog twice.
K5, (yo, k1) 7 times, k6, k2tog twice, slm, k2tog.
K6, (yo, k1) 5 times, k14, sl3 wyif. 580 sts.

Only continue with Wedge 4 if you used 355yds / 325m or less of color A in SECTION 1.
If you used more than 355yds / 325m of color A in SECTION 1 and you still want to continue with Wedge 4, you could use an additional color pop!

Wedge 4
Row 1 (RS): K to last 3 sts, sl3 wyif.
Row 2 (WS): K to last stitch marker, slm, k1, turn to work RS.

Row 3 (RS): K to last 3 sts, sl3 wyif.
Row 4 (WS): K to the stitch marker before the previous short row turn, slm, k1, turn to work RS.

Repeat Rows 3 & 4 6 more times. You will be turning around 1 stitch marker earlier each time.

Row 17 (RS): K to last 3 sts, sl3 wyif.
Row 18 (WS): K73, (yo, k1) 25 times, k20, k2tog 9 times, slm, k2tog 8 times.
K13, (yo, k1) 23 times, k24, k2tog 7 times, slm, k2tog 6 times.
K16, (yo, k1) 21 times, k20, k2tog 6 times, slm, k2tog 5 times.
K14, (yo, k1) 17 times, k20, k2tog 4 times, slm, k2tog 3 times.
K15, (yo, k1) 13 times, k12, k2tog 4 times, slm, k2tog 3 times.
K10, (yo, k1) 11 times, k13, k2tog 3 times, slm, k2tog twice.
K11, (yo, k1) 9 times, k13, k2tog twice, slm, k2tog twice.
K6, (yo, k1) 7 times, k8, k2tog twice, slm, k2tog.
K7, (yo, k1) 5 times, k17, sl3 wyif. 644 sts.

There shouldn't be much yarn remaining after SECTIONS 1-3. Section 4 will be very flexible so you won't need much more yarn to complete the shawl. If you have more yarn, then there will be options in the next section to add more colors.

SECTION 4
Select from the 3 different border options to finish The Doodler. Read the sentences below each option to determine which choice is best for you.
You can break color C if you continue to work your border option with color B. Each option continues with the stitches from SECTION 3. If you added a fourth color to your Doodler or you want to add an additional color to your Doodler now, then these border options are a great chance to use additional color pops!

Option #1 - I-cord Bind Off
Uses approximately 60yds / 55m of color B. Immediately bind off your stitches with the instructions below if you are ready for a quick finish to your shawl. This option uses the least amount of yarn. I recommend using color B, but feel free to use any color for the final edging.

Row 1 (RS): Using color B, k to last 3 sts, sl3 wyif.

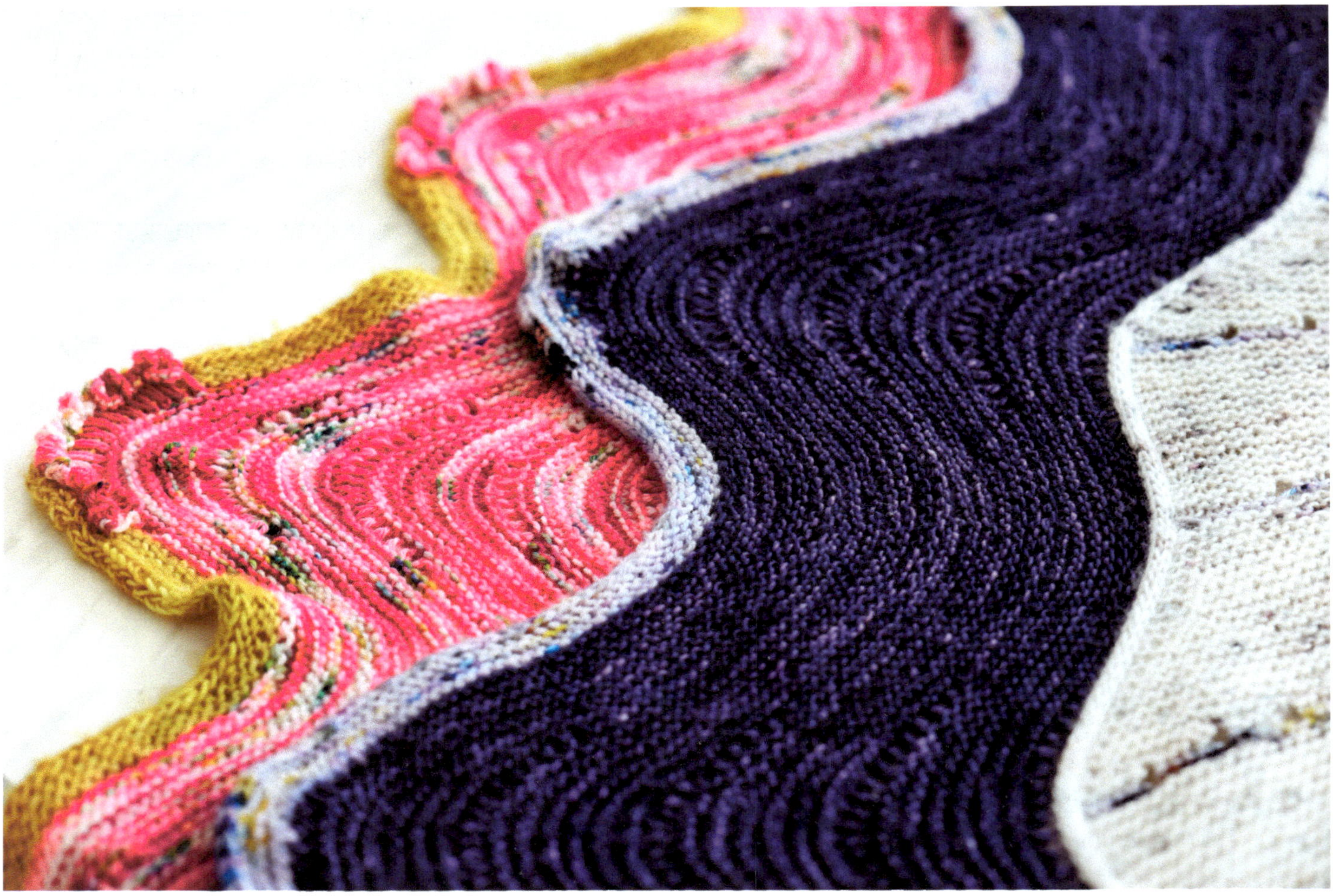

BO all sts on the next WS row as follows, *k2, k2tog tbl, slip 3 sts onto left needle, repeat form * to last 3 sts. Graft the remaining 6 total sts together using kitchener stitch for a seamless finish.

Break yarn, weave in ends, and block your finished shawl.

Option #2 - Garter Stitch Border & I-cord Bind Off
Uses approximately 110yds / 100m of color B. Work a garter stitch border with the instructions below. I recommend working 6 rows with color B before binding off. If you have more colors, feel free to add additional rows and colorful stripes to your border. This option is ideal for using leftover bits of yarn if you choose to add color A and/or C to any of the rows.

Row 1 (RS): Using color B, k to last 3 sts, sl3 wyif.
Row 2 (WS): K to last 3 sts, sl3 wyif.

Repeat last 2 rows twice more. There should be 3 color B garter ridges unless you decide to add additional rows and stripes. Make it your own!

BO all sts on the next RS row as follows, *k2, k2tog tbl, slip 3 sts onto left needle, repeat form * to last 3 sts. Graft the remaining 6 total sts together using kitchener stitch for a seamless finish.

Break yarn, weave in ends, and block your finished shawl.

Option #3 - Garter Stitch Border with Embellished Picot Scallops & I-cord Bind Off
Uses approximately 110yds / 100m of color B and a small amount of color C for the picot clusters.
This fancy edging decorates the border with slipped stitches, a color B stripe, and clusters of picots on each scallop using color C.

You will use color B for 6 rows and an I-cord bind off. Color C is only used for the little picot clusters on each scallop.

Row 1 instructions are on separate lines of the page for easy reading. Slipped stitches are always slipped purl-wise.

THERE ARE 2 SETS OF INSTRUCTIONS FOR ROW 1 DEPENDING ON THE NUMBER OF WEDGES YOU WORKED IN SECTION 3.
Work the first Row 1 option if you made **3 wedges** in SECTION 3 and you have **580 sts**. Work the second Row 1 option if you made **4 wedges** in SECTION 3 and you have **644 sts**.

Row 1 (RS) IF YOU WORKED 3 WEDGES IN SECTION 3: Using color B, k17, pm, (sl1 wyib, k1) 5 times, sl1 wyib, pm.
K6, remove m, k8, pm, (sl1 wyib, k1) 7 times, sl1 wyib, pm.
K6, remove m, k12, pm, (sl1 wyib, k1) 9 times, sl1 wyib, pm.
K10, remove m, k13, pm, (sl1 wyib, k1) 11 times, sl1 wyib, pm.
K10, remove m, k13, pm, (sl1 wyib, k1) 13 times, sl1 wyib, pm.
K14, remove m, k19, pm, (sl1 wyib, k1) 17 times, sl1 wyib, pm.
K15, remove m, k21, pm, (sl1 wyib, k1) 21 times, sl1 wyib, pm.
K17, remove m, k26, pm, (sl1 wyib, k1) 23 times, sl1 wyib, pm.
K17, remove m, k25, pm, (sl1 wyib, k1) 25 times, sl1 wyib, pm.
K57, sl3 wyif.

Skip ahead to Row 2 (WS).

Row 1 (RS) IF YOU WORKED 4 WEDGES IN SECTION 3: Using color B, k20, pm, (sl1 wyib, k1) 5 times, sl1 wyib, pm.
K7, remove m, k10, pm, (sl1 wyib, k1) 7 times, sl1 wyib, pm.
K7, remove m, k15, pm, (sl1 wyib, k1) 9 times, sl1 wyib, pm.

K12, remove m, k16, pm, (sl1 wyib, k1) 11 times, sl1 wyib, pm.
K12, remove m, k16, pm, (sl1 wyib, k1) 13 times, sl1 wyib, pm.
K17, remove m, k24, pm, (sl1 wyib, k1) 17 times, sl1 wyib, pm.
K18, remove m, k26, pm, (sl1 wyib, k1) 21 times, sl1 wyib, pm.
K21, remove m, k31, pm, (sl1 wyib, k1) 23 times, sl1 wyib, pm.
K20, remove m, k29, pm, (sl1 wyib, k1) 25 times, sl1 wyib, pm.
K69, sl3 wyif.

Continue working Row 2 (WS).

Row 2 (WS): *K to m, slm, sl1 wyif, (k1, sl1 wyif) to m, slm, repeat from * 8 more times, k to last 3 sts, sl3 wyif.

Row 3 (RS): *K to m, slm, sl1 wyib, (k1, sl1 wyib) to m, slm, repeat from * 8 more times, k to last 3 sts, sl3 wyif.

Repeat rows 2 & 3 once more, then repeat Row 2 (WS) once more. There should be 3 color B garter ridges.

Your 9 clusters should look like this.

Before proceeding with Next Row (RS), cut 9 strands of waste yarn. Thread a strand of waste yarn through each cluster of color C slipped sts.

Use this video to assist with the I-cord bind off.
https://youtu.be/aVnGpbGc7Ag

Next Row (RS): Using color B, *k2, k2tog tbl, slip 3 B sts onto left needle, repeat from * to 1 st before m, k2, k2tog tbl, remove m, slip 3 B sts onto left needle. **K3, slide the next color C slip stitch off the needle, slip 3 B sts onto left needle, k2, k2tog tbl, slip 3 B sts onto left needle, repeat from ** to 1 st before m, k3, slide the next color C slip stitch off the needle, remove m, slip 3 B sts onto left needle.

Continue working I-cord BO by repeating this entire row from the beginning until you reach the last 3 sts. Graft the remaining 6 total sts together using kitchener stitch for a seamless finish.

Use this video to assist with the Picot Clusters. https://youtu.be/fj7NeLNGYRg

Picot Clusters
Row 1 (RS): Using color C and with RS facing, slip a cluster of color C sts onto your needle. *K1, pick up and k1 from the color B garter ridge (the third ridge underneath the I-cord BO), repeat from * to last st, k1. Turn to work WS.

Row 2 (WS): *CO 3 sts using the cable CO, BO 6, repeat from * until all sts are bound off. Break yarn.

Repeat Rows 1 & 2 for each cluster of color C sts. 9 clusters total.

FINISHING
Break yarn, weave in ends, and block your finished shawl.

VERTICES
UNITE

49

VERTICES UNITE

Vertices Unite is a geometric shawl that combines modular knitting and playful color combinations. Increases, decreases, and short rows form the simple shapes. Each section is picked up and knit from the last section or knit while simultaneously being attached to the previous sections. An I-cord border adds a crisp outline to the finished shawl. Grab a collection of colors and choose the small or large size.

Sizes: Small [Large]

Finished Measurements: 52 [100]" / 132 [254]cm wingspan length, 14 [23]" /36 [58]cm wide. Measurements taken after blocking.

Yarn: Fingering weight

Shown in: Small Size (gray/blue/green)
Skein Top Draw Socks (85% Merino Wool, 15% Nylon; 437yds / 400m per 95g skein)
Color A - Graphite (Dark Blue)
Malabrigo Sock (100% Merino Wool; 440yds / 402m per 100g skein)
Color B - Alcaucil (Dark Green)
Madelinetosh Tosh Merino Light (100% Merino Wool; 420yds / 384m per 115g skein)
Color C - Antler (White), Color D - Dust Bowl (Gray), Color E - Oak (Yellow Green)

Large Size (turquoise border)
La Bien Aimée Merino Singles (100% Merino Wool; 400yds / 366m per 100g skein)
Color A - Namu
Color B - LBA Yellow
Color C - Lipstick
Color D - Sea Glass
Color E - Tang

Yardage: Color A - 150 [285]yds / 137 [261]m
Color B - 155 [320]yds / 142 [293]m
Color C - 90 [165]yds / 82 [151]m
Color D - 95 [230]yds / 87 [210]m
Color E - 135 [310]yds / 123 [283]m

Needles: 40" US 4 / 3.5mm circular

Notions: Tapestry needle

Gauge: 24 sts & 48 rows = 4" / 10cm in garter stitch

Large Size
5 colors

Small Size
5 colors

Section 5
A - Dark Blue
C - White

Section 4
D - Gray

BORDER
D - Gray

Section 1
A - Dark Blue
B - Dark Green

Section 6
B - Dark Green

Section 3
E - Yellow Green

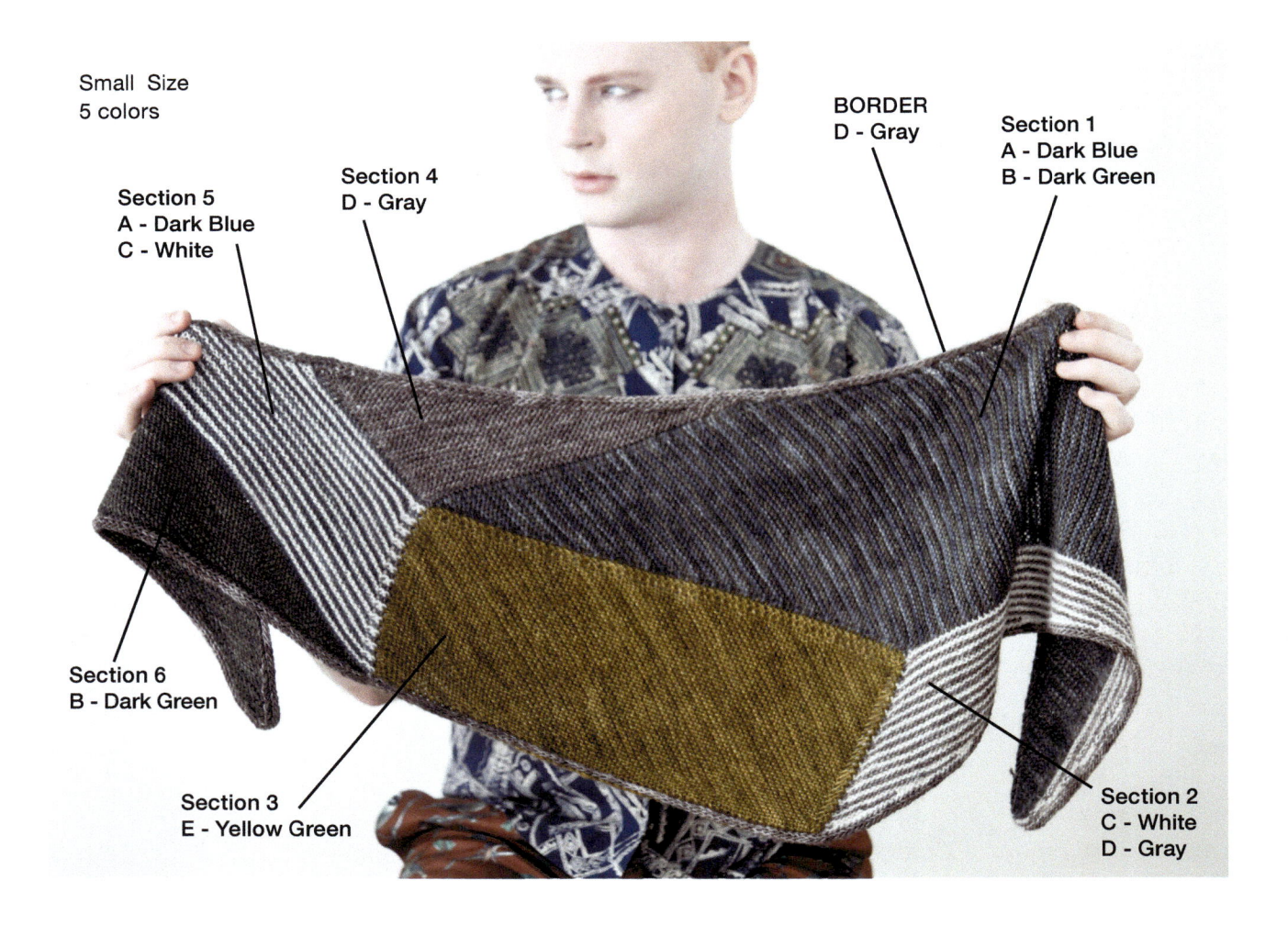

Section 2
C - White
D - Gray

INSTRUCTIONS
SECTION 1
Using A, CO 2 sts.

Row 1 (RS): Kfb, sl1 wyif.
Row 2 (WS): K2, sl1 wyif.

Row 3 (RS): Using B, k2, sl1 wyif.
Row 4 (WS): K2, sl1 wyif.

Row 5 (RS): Using A, Kfb, k to last st, sl1 wyif.
Row 6 (WS): K to last st, sl1 wyif.

Row 7 (RS): Using B, k to last st, sl1 wyif.
Row 8 (WS): K to last st, sl1 wyif.

Repeat last 4 rows 56 [86] more times. 60 [90] sts. Place a marker into the last color B garter ridge. This marks where you will start picking up stitches in SECTION 2.

Next Row (RS): Using A, k to last st, sl1 wyif.
Next Row (WS): K1, ssk, k to last st, sl1 wyif.

Next Row (RS): Using B, k to last st, sl1 wyif.
Next Row (WS): K1, ssk, k to last st, sl1 wyif.

Repeat last 4 rows 27 [42] more times. 4 sts.

Next Row (RS): Using A, k3, sl1 wyif.
Next Row (WS): K1, ssk, sl1 wyif. 3 sts.

Next Row (RS): Using B, k2, sl1 wyif.
Next Row (WS): Ssk, sl1 wyif. Break yarn and pull strand through the remaining 2 sts.

SECTION 2

Using C and with RS facing pick up and k117 [177] sts into the left SECTION 1 selvedge. Pick up sts starting at the marked color B selvedge row from SECTION 1 (before the decrease rows).

Next Row (WS): K to last st, sl1 wyif.

Row 1 (RS): Using D, kfb, k to last 5 sts, turn to work WS.
Row 2 (WS): K to last st, sl1 wyif.

Row 3 (RS): Using C, kfb, k to 5 sts before last turn, turn to work WS.
Row 4 (WS): K to last st, sl1 wyif.

Row 5 (RS): Using D, kfb, k to 5 sts before last turn, turn to work WS.
Row 6 (WS): K to last st, sl1 wyif.

Repeat last 4 rows 9 [16] more times. There should be 11 [18] color C ridges and 11 [18] color D ridges.

Next Row (RS): Using C, kfb, k to 6 [4] sts before last turn, turn to work WS.
Next Row (WS): K to last st, sl1 wyif.

Next Row (RS): Using D, kfb, k to 6 [4] sts before last turn, turn to work WS.
Next Row (WS): K to last st, sl1 wyif.

Repeat last 4 rows 2 [4] more times. Break color D.

Next Row (RS): Using C, kfb, k to last st while closing the short row gaps, sl1 wyif.
Next Row (WS): K to last st, sl1 wyif.

Break yarn and place 145 [223] sts onto waste yarn or a spare circular needle.

SECTION 3

Using E and with RS facing, pick up and k2 sts in the corner where SECTION 1 and SECTION 2 meet.

Next Row (WS): Kfb, k1. 3 sts.

Row 1 (RS): Sl1 wyif then place the yarn in back to knit, m1, k1, m1, sl2 wyif (last st & next selvedge stitch from SECTION 2). 5 sts.

Row 2 (WS): K2tog, k3, ssk (last st together with next selvedge st from SECTION 1).

Row 3 (RS): Sl1 wyif then place the yarn in back to knit, kfb twice, k1, sl2 (last st & next selvedge stitch from SECTION 2). 7 sts.
Row 4 (WS): K2tog, k to last st, ssk (last st together with next selvedge st from SECTION 1).

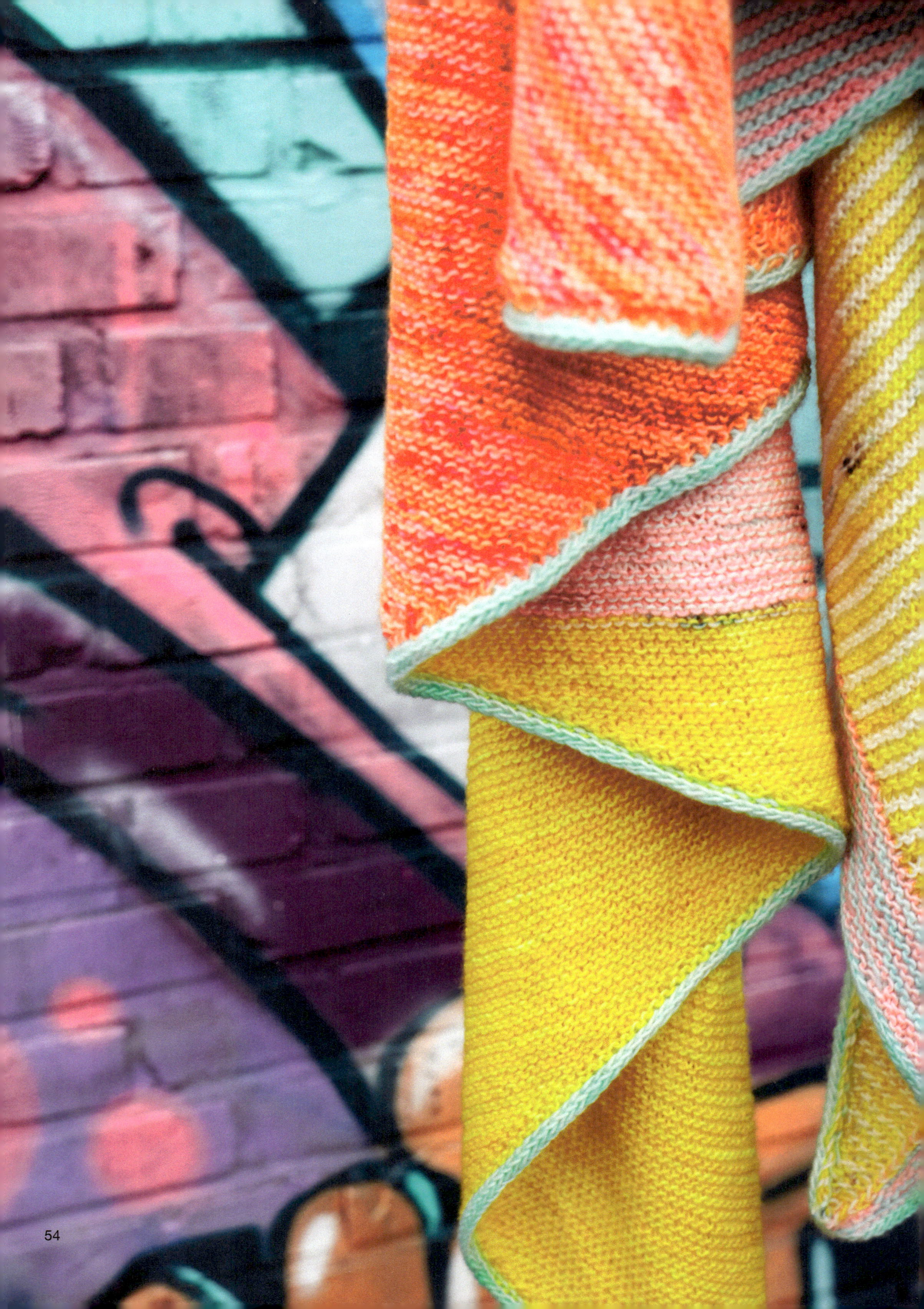

Row 5 (RS): Sl1 wyif then place the yarn in back to knit, kfb, k to last 3 sts, kfb, k1, sl2 (last st & next selvedge stitch from SECTION 2).
Row 6 (WS): K2tog, k to last st, ssk (last st together with next selvedge st from SECTION 1).

Repeat last 2 rows 25 [43] more times. 59 [95] sts.

Next Row (RS): Sl1 wyif then place the yarn in back to knit, kfb, k to last st, sl1 wyif.
Next Row (WS): K1, ssk, k to last st, ssk (last st together with next selvedge st from SECTION 1).

Repeat last 2 rows 28 [41] more times.

Next Row (RS): K to last st, sl1 wyif.
Next Row (WS): K1, ssk, k to last 3 sts, k2tog, sl1 wyif.

Repeat last 2 rows 26 [44] more times. 5 sts.

Next Row (RS): K4, sl1 wyif.
Next Row (WS): K1, SK2P, sl1 wyif.

Next Row (RS): K2, sl1 wyif.
Next Row (WS): Ssk, sl1 wyif. Break yarn and pull strand through the remaining 2 sts.

SECTION 4
Using D and with RS facing, pick up and k60 [88] sts along right edge of SECTION 1 selvedge (starting at the marked color B ridge before the SECTION 1 decreases).

Next Row (WS): K to last 2 sts, turn to work RS row.

Row 1 (RS): K to last st, sl1 wyif.
Row 2 (WS): K to 2 sts before last turn, turn to work RS.

Repeat last 2 rows 27 [41] more times.

Next Row (RS): K2, sl1 wyif.
Next Row (WS): K to last st while closing the short row gaps, sl1 wyif.

Break yarn and place 60 [88] sts onto waste yarn or a spare circular needle.

SECTION 5
Using A, pick up and k30 [44] sts into SECTION 4 selvedge, sl1 selvedge st from SECTION 3 wyif.

Next Row (WS): K2tog, k28 [42], sl1 wyif.

Row 1 (RS): Using C, kfb, k to last 3 sts, kfb, k1, sl2 wyif (last st and next selvedge st from SECTION 3).
Row 2 (WS): K2tog, k to last st, sl1 wyif.

Row 3 (RS): Using A, k to last 3 sts, kfb, k1, sl2 wyif (last st and next selvedge st from SECTION 3).
Row 4 (WS): K2tog, k to last st, sl1 wyif.

Repeat last 4 rows 13 [22] more times. 72 [113] sts. Break colors A & C.

SECTION 6
Using B, kfb, k to last st, sl1 wyif. 73 [114] sts.

Next Row (WS): K to last st, sl1 wyif.

Row 1 (RS): K to 2 sts before end of row, turn to work WS.
Row 2 (WS): K to last st, sl1 wyif.

Row 3 (RS): Kfb, k to 2 sts before last turn, turn to work WS.
Row 4 (WS): K to last st, sl1 wyif.

Row 5 (RS): K to 2 sts before last turn, turn to work WS.
Row 6 (WS): K to last st, sl1 wyif.

Repeat last 4 rows 22 [35] more times. 96 [150] sts.

Next Row (RS): Kfb, k to last st while closing the short row gaps, sl1 wyif.
Next Row (WS): K to last st, sl1 wyif. Break yarn.

BORDER

Using D or any other color for the I-cord perimeter, k all live sts and pick up and k all selvedge sts around the shawl's perimeter. Begin by knitting all SECTION 6 sts, then pick up and k1 st into each selvedge st along SECTION 3 edge, k all SECTION 2 sts, pick up and k1 st into each selvedge st along SECTION 1 edge, k all SECTION 4 sts, pick up and k1 st into each selvedge st along SECTION 5 & 6 edge.

BO all sts using an I-cord BO as follows, CO 3 sts using the cable CO method, *k2, k2tog tbl, place 3 sts back onto left needle, repeat from * until all sts are bound off.

Weave in ends and block finished garment to smooth the fabric.

57

STRIPED BOLTING

59

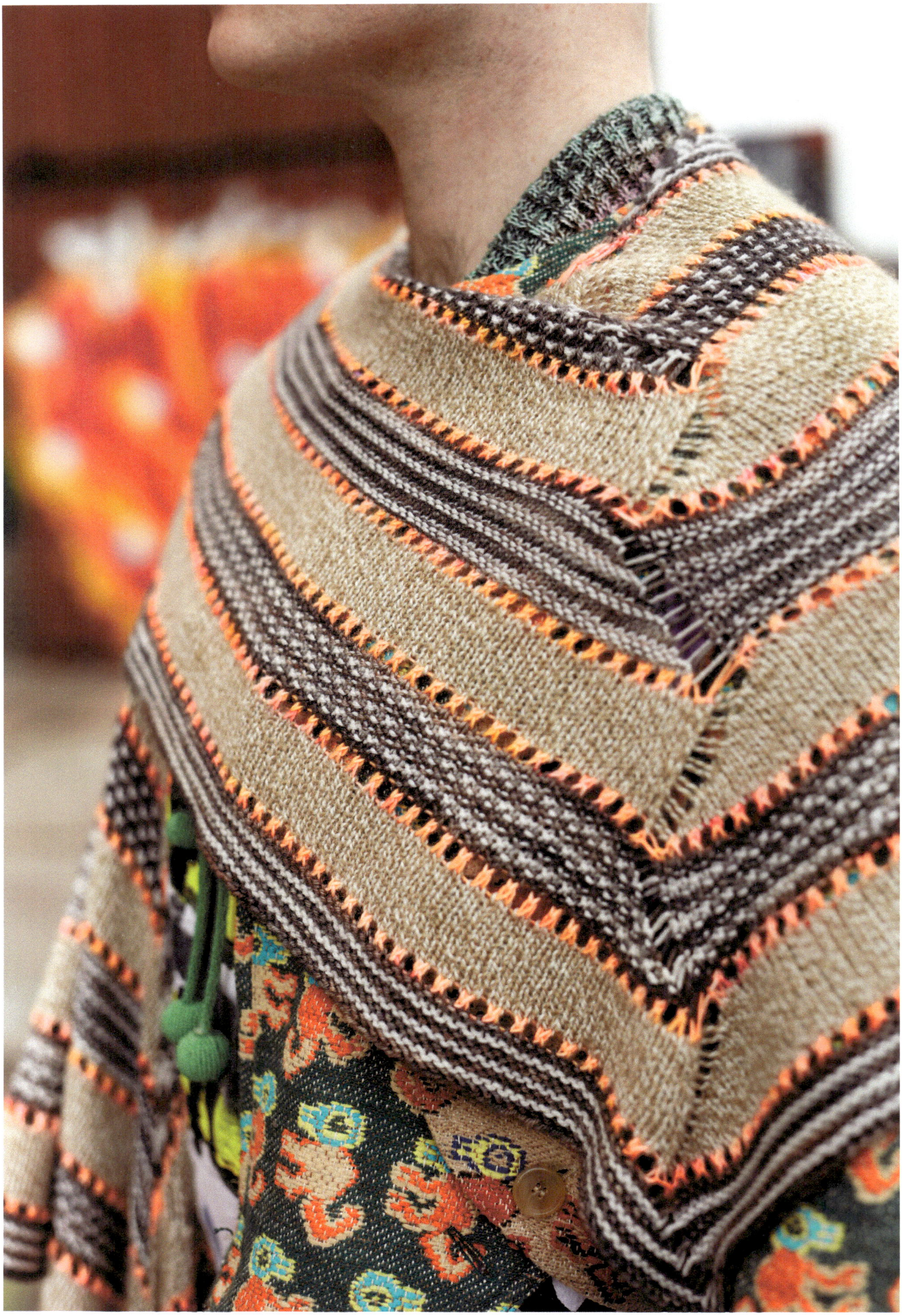

STRIPED BOLTING

This top-down geometric shawl is knit with four colors. Yarn over increases zig and zag to create the large expansive shape. Garter stitch stripes, slipped stitches, seed stitch, and eyelet rows decorate the fabric. The signature Westknits shaping style is super versatile to wear. Wrap it like a scarf or drape it over your shoulders like a poncho and rock this dramatic statement piece.

Finished Measurements: 100" / 254cm wingspan from tip to tip, 26" / 66cm along center point from CO to BO edges. Measurements taken after blocking.

Yarn: Fingering weight

Shown in: Beige Version
Woolfolk Sno (100% Ultimate Merino; 223yds / 204m per 50g skein)
Color A - 1 + 7 Snow & Medium Bronze (marled beige & cream)

La Bien Aimée Merino Singles (100% Merino Wool; 400yds / 366m per 100g skein)
Color B - Tang (orange)

La Bien Aimée Ultimate Merino Fingering (394yds / 360m per 100g skein)
Color C - Soubois (dark grey)
Color D - French Grey (light grey)

Black & White Version
Woolfolk Sno (100% Ultimate Merino; 223yds / 204m per 50g skein)
Color A - 1 + 15 Snow & Black

Woolfolk Tynd (100% Ultimate Merino; 223yds / 204m per 50g skein)
Color C - 01 Sno (substituted a white mohair yarn in section 4)
Color D - 05 Raven (substituted a black eyelash novelty yarn in section 3)

Shibui Linen (100% Linen; 246yds / 225m per 50g skein) Color B - 2026 Brass

Yardage: Color A - 500yds / 457m
Color B - 160yds / 146m
Color C - 390yds / 357m
Color D - 280yds / 265m

Needles: 60" US 6 / 4mm circular

Notions: 5 stitch markers, tapestry needle

Gauge: 19 sts & 25 rows = 4" / 10cm in stockinette stitch

Pattern Notes: C16B: (cable 16 back) slip 8 stitches onto cable needle or DPN and hold in back of work, knit 8, knit 8 stitches from cable needle or DPN.
Stitches increase throughout Section 2, so the cables will increase to C18B, C20B, C22B, etc… Always place the first half of the stitches onto cable needle or DPN and hold them in back. For example, C24B: slip 12 stitches onto cable needle and hold in back of work, knit 12 stitches, knit 12 stitches from cable needle or DPN.

INSTRUCTIONS
SECTION 1

Using A, CO 3 sts. K7 rows.

At the end of last row, do not turn to work other side, rotate piece 90 degrees clockwise so that you are looking at the long side of the garter rectangle. Pick up and k3 sts in the purl bump of each garter ridge. Rotate piece another 90 degrees. Pick up and k3 sts along the CO edge. 9 sts. Turn to work WS row.

Set Up Row (WS): K3, yo, p1, yo, pm, p1tbl, p1, yo, k3.

Row 1 (RS): K3, yo, k to 1 st before m, k1tbl, slm, yo, k to last 3 sts, yo, k3.
Row 2 (WS): K3, yo, p to m, yo, slm, p1tbl, p to last 3 sts, yo, k3.

Repeat last 2 rows 6 more times. 54 sts. Break color A.

Row 15 (RS): Using B, k3, yo, k to 1 st before m, k1tbl, slm, yo, k to last 3 sts, yo, k3.
Row 16 (WS): K3, yo, k1, (yo, k2tog) to m, yo, slm, k1tbl, (yo, k2tog) to last 4 sts, k1, yo, k3. 60 sts. Break color B.

Row 17 (RS): Using C, k3, yo, k to m, yo, slm, k1tbl, k to last 3 sts, yo, k3.
Row 18 (WS): K3, yo, k to 1 st before m, k1tbl, slm, yo, k to last 3 sts, yo, k3.

Row 19 (RS): Using D, k3, yo, k to m, yo, slm, k1tbl, k to last 3 sts, yo, k3.
Row 20 (WS): K3, yo, k to 1 st before m, k1tbl, slm, yo, k to last 3 sts, yo, k3.

Repeat last 4 rows 2 more times then repeat Rows 17 & 18 once more. There should be 4 color C stripes. 102 sts. Break colors C & D.

Next Row (RS): Using B, k3, yo, k to m, yo, slm, k1tbl, k to last 3 sts, yo, k3.
Next Row (WS): K3, yo, k1, (yo, k2tog) to 1 st before m, k1tbl, slm, yo, k1, (yo, k2tog) to last 3 sts, yo, k3. 108 sts. Break color B.

SECTION 2

Row 1 (RS): Using A, k3, yo, k1tbl, pm, yo, k to 1 st before m, k1tbl, slm, yo, k to last 5 sts, k1tbl, pm, yo, k1, yo, k3.
Row 2 (WS): K3, yo, (p to m, yo, slm, p1tbl) 3 times, p to last 3 sts, yo, k3. 118 sts.

Row 3 (RS): K3, yo, (k to 1 st before m, k1tbl, slm, yo) 3 times, k to last 3 sts, yo, k3.
Row 4 (WS): K3, yo, (p to m, yo, slm, p1tbl) 3 times, p to last 3 sts, yo, k3.

Repeat last 2 rows 5 more times. 178 sts. Break color A.

Row 15 (RS): Using B, k3, yo, (k to 1 st before m, k1tbl, slm, yo) 3 times, k to last 3 sts, yo, k3.
Row 16 (WS): K3, yo, k1, *(yo, k2tog) to m, yo, slm, k1tbl, repeat from * twice more, (yo, k2tog) to last 4 sts, k1, yo, k3. 188 sts. Break color B.

Row 17 (RS): Using C, k3, yo, (k to m, yo, slm, k1tbl) 3 times, k to last 3 sts, yo, k3.
Row 18 (WS): K3, yo, (p to 1 st before m, p1tbl, slm, yo) 3 times, p to last 3 sts, yo, k3.

Row 19 (RS): Using D, k3, yo, k1, *(sl1 wyib, k1) to m, yo, slm, repeat from * twice more, (sl1 wyib, k1) to last 4 sts, sl1 wyib, yo, k3.
Row 20 (WS): K3, yo, *(k1, sl1 wyif) to m, slm, yo, k1, repeat from * twice more, (k1, sl1 wyif) to last 5 sts, k2, yo, k3.

Row 21 (RS): Using C, k3, yo, (k to m, yo, slm, k1tbl) 3 times, k to last 3 sts, yo, k3.
Row 22 (WS): K3, yo, (p to 1 st before m, p1tbl, slm, yo) 3 times, p to last 3 sts, yo, k3.

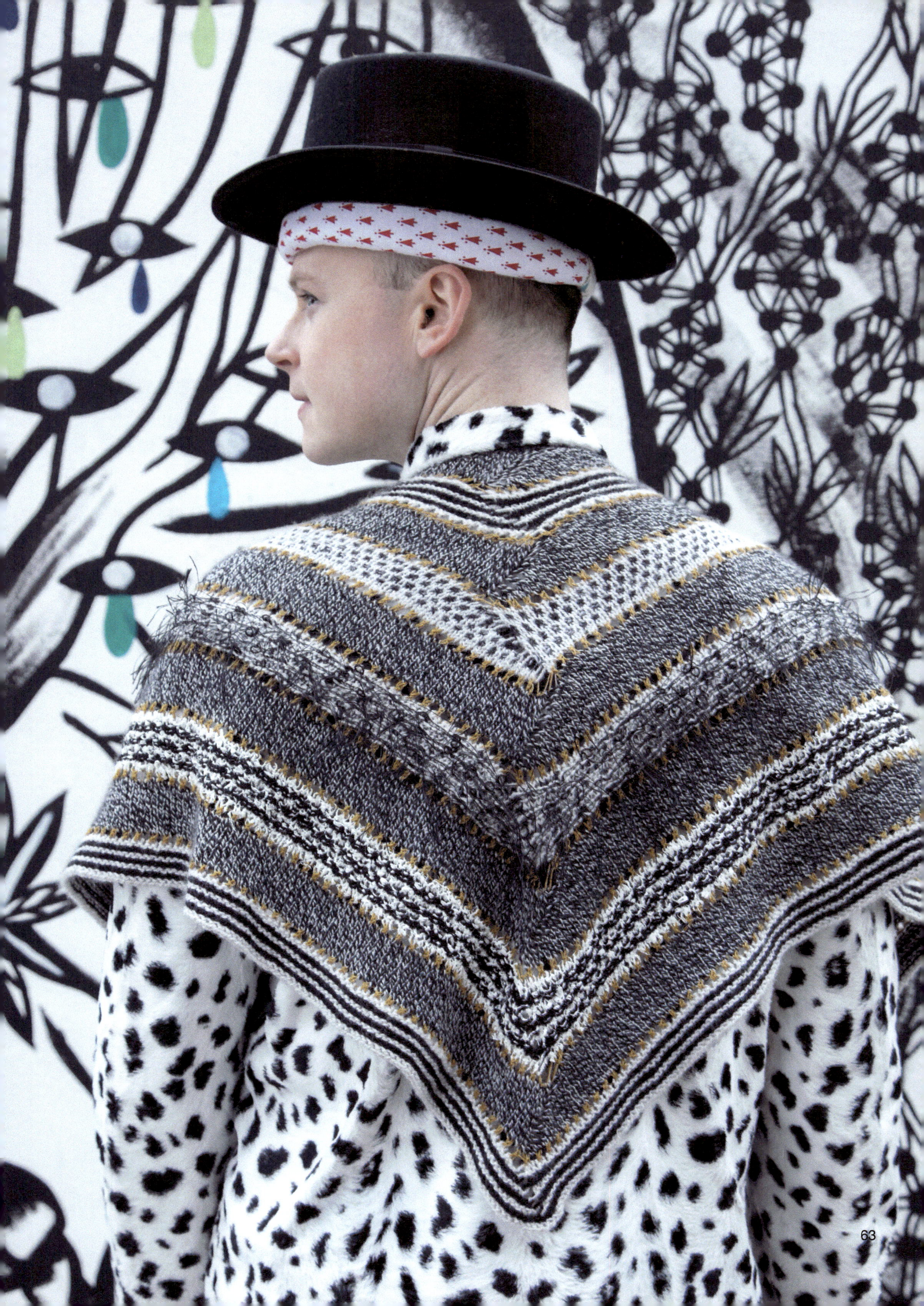

64

Row 23 (RS): Using D, k3, yo, sl1 wyib *(k1, sl1 wyib) to m, yo, slm, repeat from * twice more, (k1, sl1 wyib) to last 4 sts, k1, yo, k3.
Row 24 (WS): K3, yo, k2, *(sl1 wyif, k1) to m, slm, yo, k1, repeat from * twice more, (sl1 wyif, k1) to last 3 sts, yo, k3.

Repeat Rows 17-24 once more then repeat Row 17 once more. There should be 4 color D stripes. 273 sts. Break colors C & D.
At the end of last Row 17 (RS), do not turn to work WS. Instead, slide sts to work the same RS row with color B.

Next Row (RS): Using B, k3, yo, (k to m, yo, slm, k1tbl) 3 times, k to last 3 sts, yo, k3.
Next Row (WS): K3, yo, k1, (yo, k2tog) to m, slm, yo, k1, *(yo, k2tog) to 1 st before m, k1tbl, slm, yo, k1, repeat from * once more, (yo, k2tog) to last 3 sts, yo, k3. 283 sts. Break color B.

SECTION 3
Row 1 (RS): Using A, k3, yo, k1tbl, pm, yo, (k to 1 st before m, k1tbl, slm, yo) 3 times, k to last 5 sts, k1tbl, pm, yo, k1, yo, k3.
Row 2 (WS): K3, yo, (p to m, yo, slm, p1tbl) 5 times, p to last 3 sts, yo, k3. 297 sts.

Row 3 (RS): K3, yo, (k to 1 st before m, k1tbl, slm, yo) 5 times, k to last 3 sts, yo, k3.
Row 4 (WS): K3, yo, (p to m, yo, slm, p1tbl) 5 times, p to last 3 sts, yo, k3.

Repeat last 2 rows 5 more times. 381 sts. Break color A.

Row 15 (RS): Using color B, k3, yo, (k to 1 st before m, k1tbl, slm, yo) 5 times, k to last 3 sts, yo, k3.
Row 16 (WS): K3, yo, k1, (yo, k2tog) to m, yo, slm, k1tbl, *(yo, k2tog) to 1 st before m, k1, yo, slm, k1tbl, repeat from * 2 more times, (yo, k2tog) to m, yo, slm, k1tbl (yo, k2tog) to last 4 sts, k1, yo, k3. 395 sts. Break color B.

Row 17 (RS): Using C, k3, yo, *k to m, yo, slm, k1tbl, repeat from * 4 more times, k to last 3 sts, yo, k3. Do not turn work. Slide sts to work the RS again with color D.
Row 18 (RS): Using D, k3, yo, *k to m, yo, slm, k1tbl, repeat from * 4 more times, k to last 3 sts, yo, k3. Turn to work WS.

Row 19 (WS): Using C, k3, yo, *k to 1 st before m, k1tbl, slm, yo, repeat from * 4 more times, k to last 3 sts, yo, k3. Do not turn work. Slide sts to work the WS again with color D.
Row 20 (WS): Using D, k3, yo, *k to 1 st before m, k1tbl, slm, yo, repeat from * 4 more times, k to last 3 sts, yo, k3. Turn to work RS.

Repeat last 4 rows 3 more times. 507 sts. Break colors C & D.

Next Row (RS): Using B, k3, yo, *k to m, yo, slm, k1tbl, repeat from * 4 more times, k to last 3 sts, yo, k3.
Next Row (WS): K3, yo, k1, *(yo, k2tog) to 1 st before m, ktbl, slm, yo, k1, repeat from * 3 more times, (yo, k2tog) to m, slm, yo, k1 (yo, k2tog) to last 3 sts, yo, k3. 521 sts. Break color B.

SECTION 4
Row 1 (RS): Using A, k3, yo, (k to 1 st before m, k1tbl, slm, yo) 5 times, k to last 3 sts, yo, k3.
Row 2 (WS): K3, yo, (p to m, yo, slm, p1tbl) 5 times, p to last 3 sts, yo, k3.

Repeat last 2 rows 6 more times. Break color A. 619 sts.

Row 15 (RS): Using color B, k3, yo, (k to 1 st before m, k1tbl, slm, yo) 5 times, k to last 3 sts, yo, k3.
Row 16 (WS): K3, yo, k1, (yo, k2tog) to m, yo, slm, k1tbl, *(yo, k2tog) to 1 st before m, k1, yo, slm, k1tbl, repeat from * 2 more times, (yo, k2tog) to m, yo, slm, k1tbl (yo, k2tog) to last 4 sts, k1, yo, k3. 633 sts. Break color B.

Row 17 (RS): Using C, k3, yo, *k to m, yo, slm, k1tbl, repeat from * 4 more times, k to last 3 sts, yo, k3.
Row 18 (WS): K3, yo, (k1, p1) to 1 st before m, k1, slm, yo, *(k1, p1) to m, slm, yo, repeat from * 2 more times, (k1, p1) to 1 st before m, k1, slm, yo, (k1, p1) to last 4 sts, k1, yo, k3.

Row 19 (RS): Using D, k3, yo, (p1, k1) to 1 st before m, p1, yo, slm, (k1, p1) to m, yo, slm, *(p1, k1) to 1 st before m, p1, yo, slm, repeat from * 2 more times, (k1, p1) to last 3 sts, yo, k3.
Row 20 (WS): K3, yo, (k1, p1) to 1 st before m, k1, slm, yo, *(k1, p1) to m, slm, yo, repeat from * 2 more times, (k1, p1) to 1 st before m, k1, slm, yo, (k1, p1) to last 4 sts, k1, yo, k3.

Using color C, repeat Rows 19 & 20 once more. Continue working Rows 19 & 20 alternating colors D & C for 2 rows each until there are a total of 4 color C stripes and 3 color D stripes. 731 sts.

Next Row (RS): Using B, k3, yo, *k to m, yo, slm, k1tbl, repeat from * 4 more times, k to last 3 sts, yo, k3.
Next Row (WS): K3, yo, k1, (yo, k2tog) to m, slm, yo, k1, *(yo, k2tog) to 1 st before m, k1tbl, slm, yo, k1, repeat from * 2 more times, (yo, k2tog) to m, slm, yo, k1 (yo, k2tog) to last 3 sts, yo, k3. Break color B. 745 sts.

SECTION 5
Row 1 (RS): Using A, k3, yo, (k to 1 st before m, k1tbl, slm, yo) 5 times, k to last 3 sts, yo, k3.
Row 2 (WS): K3, yo, (p to m, yo, slm, p1tbl) 5 times, p to last 3 sts, yo, k3.

Repeat last 2 rows 6 more times. Break color A. 843 sts.

Row 15 (RS): Using color B, k3, yo, (k to 1 st before m, k1tbl, slm, yo) 5 times, k to last 3 sts, yo, k3.
Row 16 (WS): K3, yo, k1, *(yo, k2tog) to 1 st before m, k1, yo, slm, k1tbl, repeat from * 3 more times, (yo, k2tog) to m, yo, slm, k1tbl (yo, k2tog) to last 4 sts, k1, yo, k3. 857 sts. Break color B.

Row 17 (RS): Using C, k3, yo, (k to m, yo, slm, k1tbl) 5 times, k to last 3 sts, yo, k3.
Row 18 (WS): K3, yo, (k to 1 st before m, k1tbl, slm, yo) 5 times, k to last 3 sts, yo, k3.

Row 19 (RS): Using D, k3, yo, (k to m, yo, slm, k1tbl) 5 times, k to last 3 sts, yo, k3.
Row 20 (WS): K3, yo, (k to 1 st before m, k1tbl, slm, yo) 5 times, k to last 3 sts, yo, k3.

Repeat last 4 rows 2 more times then repeat Rows 17 & 18 once more. There should be 4 color C stripes. 955 sts.

FINISHING

Using color C, BO all sts loosely on next RS row as follows, (k2tog tbl, slip stitch onto to left needle) to end of row. Break yarn and pull it through the last stitch. Weave in ends and block the shawl to desired measurements.

STARBURST

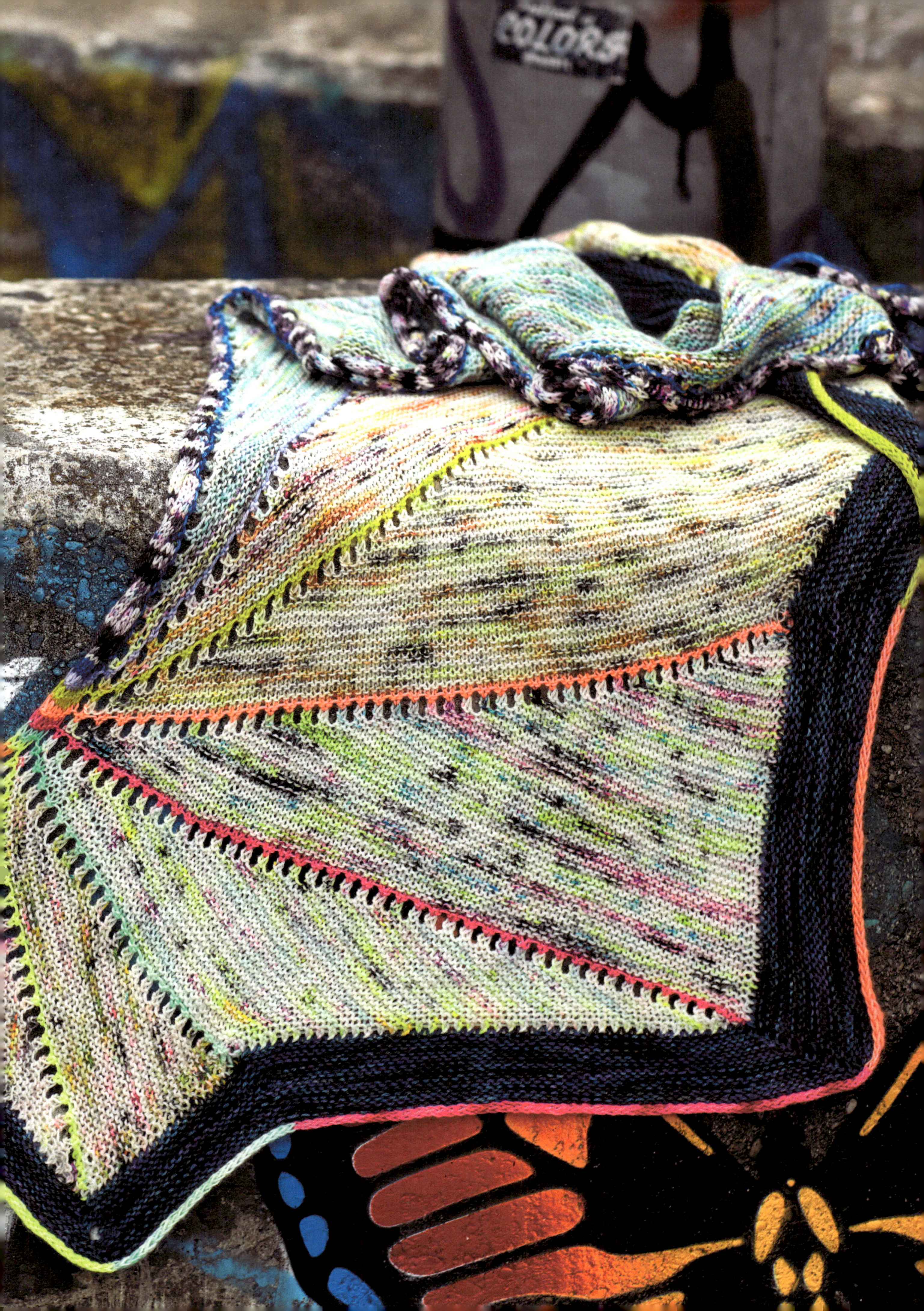
COLORS

Large Size

STARBURST

Choose all your favorite speckled yarns and knit the large shlanket (shawl + blanket) of your dreams or select three colors for a small version. Short row wedges with colorful stripes form the starburst shape. Pick up stitches and knit along the border to accentuate the jagged edge. A tiny cable completes the shawl with a decorative finish.

Sizes: Small [Large]

Finished Measurements: 19 [28]" / 48 [71]cm from cable edge to I-cord BO measured at widest part, 78 [125]" / 198 [318]cm wingspan length. Measurements taken after blocking.

Yarn: Fingering weight

Yardage: Small Size
Color A - 300yds / 274m (short row wedges)
Colors B & D - 80yds / 73m (thin yarn over stripe & cable shown in the same orange color)
Color C - 275yds / 251m (border)

Large Size
Color A - 975yds / 892m short row wedges
Color B - 40yds / 37m thin yarn over line between short row wedges
Color C - 325yds / 297m (border)
Color D - 150yds / 137m

You will need at least 2 balls and a bit more yarn for color A. The last wedge uses an entire skein or a bit more.

Shown in: Hedgehog Fibres Sock Yarn
Small Size
Color A - Penelope (white speckle)
Color B - Kid You Not (orange)
Color C - Potluck (blue speckle)

Large Size
Color A - Each short row wedge is a different speckled color including Typewriter, Crybaby, Where's My Bike?, Boombox, and various potluck colors.
Color B - Each color B stripe is a different color including Pollen, Kid You Not, Highlighter, Skinny Dip, Jelly, Coral, Envy, Hush, and Electric.
Color C - Eel
Color D - Night Ride

Needles: 40" US 4 / 3.5mm circular

Notions: 8 stitch markers, cable needle, tapestry needle

Gauge: 22 sts & 52 rows = 4" / 10cm in garter stitch

Abbreviations:
C10B: (cable 10 back) slip 5 sts onto cable needle and hold to back of work, k5, k5 from cable needle.

INSTRUCTIONS

If you're making a multi-color version, use a new color A at the beginning of each Wedge.

SECTION 1
Using color A, CO 14 sts.

Next Row (WS): K13, sl1 wyif.

Wedge 1
Row 1 (RS): Kfb, k to last st, turn to work WS.
Row 2 (WS): K to last st, sl1 wyif.

Row 3 (RS): Kfb, k to 2 sts before last turn, turn to work WS.
Row 4 (WS): K to last st, sl1 wyif.

Repeat last 2 rows 9 more times. 25 sts. There should be 4 sts at the beginning of the row before your last short row turn.

Next Row (RS): Using color B, kfb, k1, (k2tog, yo) 11 times, sl1 wyif. 26 sts.
Next Row (WS): K to last st, sl1 wyif. Break color B.

Wedge 2
Row 1 (RS): Using color A, k to last 2 sts, turn to work WS.
Row 2 (WS): K to last st, sl1 wyif.

Row 3 (RS): K to 2 sts before last turn, turn to work WS.
Row 4 (WS): K to last st, sl1 wyif.

Repeat last 2 rows 9 more times. There should be 4 sts at the beginning of the row before your last short row turn.

Next Row (RS): Using color B, k2, (k2tog, yo) 11 times, k1, sl1 wyif.
Next Row (WS): K to last st, sl1 wyif. Break color B.

Wedge 3
Row 1 (RS): Using color A, kfb, k to last 3 sts, turn to work WS.
Row 2 (WS): K to last st, sl1 wyif.

Row 3 (RS): Kfb, k to 2 sts before last turn, turn to work WS.
Row 4 (WS): K to last st, sl1 wyif.

Repeat last 2 rows 19 more times. 47 sts. There should be 4 sts at the beginning of the row before your last short row turn.

Next Row (RS): Using color B, kfb, k1, (k2tog, yo) 21 times, k2, sl1 wyif. 48 sts.
Next Row (WS): K to last st, sl1 wyif.

Wedge 4
Row 1 (RS): Using color A, k to last 4 sts, turn to work WS.
Row 2 (WS): K to last st, sl1 wyif.

Row 3 (RS): K to 2 sts before last turn, turn to work WS.
Row 4 (WS): K to last st, sl1 wyif.

Repeat last 2 rows 19 more times. There should be 4 sts at the beginning of the row before your last short row turn.

Next Row (RS): Using color B, k2, (k2tog, yo) 21 times, k3, sl1 wyif.
Next Row (WS): K to last st, sl1 wyif. Break color B.

Wedge 5
Row 1 (RS): Using color A, kfb, k to last 5 sts, turn to work WS.
Row 2 (WS): K to last st, sl1 wyif.

Row 3 (RS): Kfb, k to 2 sts before last turn, turn to work WS.
Row 4 (WS): K to last st, sl1 wyif.

Repeat last 2 rows 39 more times. 89 sts. There should be 4 sts at the beginning of the row before your last short row turn.

Next Row (RS): Using color B, kfb, k1, (k2tog, yo) 41 times, k4, sl1 wyif. 90 sts.
Next Row (WS): K to last st, sl1 wyif. Break color B.

Wedge 6
Row 1 (RS): Using color A, k to last 6 sts, turn to work WS.
Row 2 (WS): K to last st, sl1 wyif.

Row 3 (RS): K to 2 sts before last turn, turn to work WS.
Row 4 (WS): K to last st, sl1 wyif.

Repeat last 2 rows 39 more times. There should be 4 sts at the beginning of the row before your last short row turn.

Next Row (RS): Using color B, k2, (k2tog, yo) 41 times, k5, sl1 wyif.
Next Row (WS): K to last st, sl1 wyif. Break color B.

Wedge 7
Row 1 (RS): Using color A, kfb, k to last 7 sts, turn to work WS.
Row 2 (WS): K to last st, sl1 wyif.

Row 3 (RS): Kfb, k to 2 sts before last turn, turn to work WS.
Row 4 (WS): K to last st, sl1 wyif.

Repeat last 2 rows 79 more times. 171 sts. There should be 4 sts at the beginning of the row before your last short row turn.

Next Row (RS): Using color B, kfb, k1, (k2tog, yo) 81 times, k6, sl1 wyif. 172 sts.
Next Row (WS): K to last st, sl1 wyif. Break color B.

Small Size Only
Place all sts onto a spare circular needle or leave them on the needle and use a new circular needle for SECTION 2. Break color A. Skip ahead to SECTION 2 instructions.

Large Size Only
Wedge 8
Row 1 (RS): Using color A, k to last 8 sts, turn to work WS.
Row 2 (WS): K to last st, sl1 wyif.

Row 3 (RS): K to 2 sts before last turn, turn to work WS.
Row 4 (WS): K to last st, sl1 wyif.

Repeat last 2 rows 79 more times. There should be 4 sts at the beginning of the row before your last short row turn.

Next Row (RS): Using color B, k2, (k2tog, yo) 81 times, k7, sl1 wyif.
Next Row (WS): K to last st, sl1 wyif. Break color B.

Wedge 9
Row 1 (RS): Using color A, kfb, k to last 9 sts, turn to work WS.
Row 2 (WS): K to last st, sl1 wyif.

Row 3 (RS): Kfb, k to 2 sts before last turn, turn to work WS.
Row 4 (WS): K to last st, sl1 wyif.

Repeat last 2 rows 159 more times. 333 sts. There should be 4 sts at the beginning of the row before your last short row turn. Break color A.

Next Row (RS): Using color B, kfb, k1, (k2tog, yo) 161 times, k8, sl1 wyif. 334 sts.
Next Row (WS): K to last st, sl1 wyif. Break color B.

Place all sts onto a spare circular needle or leave them on the needle and use a new circular needle for the next section.

SECTION 2 - Both Sizes
Using color C and with RS facing,
(Pick up and k3 sts from Wedge 1 selvedge, m1) 4 times. 16 sts.
Pick up and k last Wedge 1 selvedge st, place marker. 17 sts.
Pick up and k12 sts from Wedge 2 selvedge, place marker. 29 sts.
(Pick up and k3 sts from Wedge 3 selvedge, m1) 7 times. 57 sts.
Pick up and k last Wedge 3 selvedge st, place marker. 58 sts.
Pick up and k22 sts from Wedge 4 selvedge, place marker. 80 sts.
(Pick up and k3 sts from Wedge 5 selvedge, m1) 14 times, place marker. 136 sts.
Pick up and k42 sts from Wedge 6 selvedge, place marker. 178 sts.
(Pick up and k3 sts from Wedge 7 selvedge, m1) 27 times. 286 sts.
Pick up and k last Wedge 7 selvedge st. 287 sts.

Continue following Small Size instructions or skip ahead to Large Size.

Small Size Only
Turn to work WS.
Next Row (WS): Kfb, *k to 2 sts before m, k2tog, slm, k to m, slm, yo, repeat from * 2 more times, k to last 3 sts, k2tog, sl1 wyif.

In the following RS rows, slip the stitch markers onto the needle as you reach them. You will begin working short rows. For every WS row, you will turn the work one stitch marker earlier each time.

Row 1 (RS): K to last st, yo, sl1 wyif.
Row 2 (WS): Kfb, *k to 2 sts before m, k2tog, slm, k to m, slm, yo, repeat from * once more, k to 2 sts before m, k2tog, slm, k to m. Leave marker on left needle. Turn to work RS.

Row 3 (RS): K to last st, yo, sl1 wyif.
Row 4 (WS): Kfb, *k to 2 sts before m, k2tog, slm, k to m, slm, yo, repeat from * once more, k to 2 sts before m, k2tog. Leave marker on left needle. Turn to work RS.

Row 5 (RS): K to last st, yo, sl1 wyif.
Row 6 (WS): Kfb, k to 2 sts before m, k2tog, slm, k to m, slm, yo, k to 2 sts before m, k2tog, slm, k to m. Leave marker on left needle. Turn to work RS.

Row 7 (RS): K to last st, yo, sl1 wyif.
Row 8 (WS): Kfb, k to 2 sts before m, k2tog, slm, k to m, slm, yo, k to 2 sts before m, k2tog. Leave marker on left needle. Turn to work RS.

Row 9 (RS): K to last st, yo, sl1 wyif.
Row 10 (WS): Kfb, k to 2 sts before m, k2tog, slm, k to m. Leave marker on left needle. Turn to work RS.

Row 11 (RS): K to last st, yo, sl1 wyif.
Row 12 (WS): Kfb, k to 2 sts before m, k2tog. Leave marker on left needle. Turn to work RS.

Row 13 (RS): K to last st, yo, sl1 wyif.

In the next row, close the short row gap after each "k2tog, slm" by picking up the garter stitch bump with left needle, slip the picked up stitch knit-wise with right needle, slip the next stitch knit-wise with right needle, k those 2 sts together tbl.

Row 14 (WS): Kfb, *k to 2 sts before m, k2tog, slm, close short row gap, k to m, slm, yo, repeat from * 2 more times, k to last 3 sts, k2tog, sl1 wyif.

Repeat Rows 1-14 three more times. There should be 4 total color C wedges. Break color C. Place all sts onto a spare circular needle or leave them on the needle and use a new circular needle for the next section.

Skip ahead to SECTION 3 for Small Size.

Large Size Only
Pick up and k82 sts from Wedge 8 selvedge, place marker. 369 sts.

(Pick up and k3 sts from Wedge 9 selvedge, m1) 54 times. 585 sts.

Turn to work WS.
Next Row (WS): Kfb, *k to 2 sts before m, k2tog, slm, k to m, slm, yo, repeat from * 3 more times, k to last 3 sts, k2tog, sl1 wyif.

In the following RS rows, slip the stitch markers onto the needle as you reach them. You will begin working short rows. For every WS row, you will turn the work one stitch marker earlier each time.

Row 1 (RS): K to last st, yo, sl1 wyif.
Row 2 (WS): Kfb, *k to 2 sts before m, k2tog, slm, k to m, slm, yo, repeat from * twice more, k to 2 sts before m, k2tog, slm, k to m. Leave marker on left needle. Turn to work RS.

Row 3 (RS): K to last st, yo, sl1 wyif.
Row 4 (WS): Kfb, *k to 2 sts before m, k2tog, slm, k to m, slm, yo, repeat from * twice more, k to 2 sts before m, k2tog. Leave marker on left needle. Turn to work RS.

Row 5 (RS): K to last st, yo, sl1 wyif.
Row 6 (WS): Kfb, *k to 2 sts before m, k2tog, slm, k to m, slm, yo, repeat from * once more, k to 2 sts before m, k2tog, slm, k to m. Leave marker on left needle. Turn to work RS.

Row 7 (RS): K to last st, yo, sl1 wyif.
Row 8 (WS): Kfb, *k to 2 sts before m, k2tog, slm, k to m, slm, yo, repeat from * once more, k to 2 sts before m, k2tog. Leave marker on left needle. Turn to work RS.

Row 9 (RS): K to last st, yo, sl1 wyif.
Row 10 (WS): Kfb, k to 2 sts before m, k2tog, slm, k to m, slm, yo, k to 2 sts before m, k2tog, slm, k to m. Leave marker on left needle. Turn to work RS.

Row 11 (RS): K to last st, yo, sl1 wyif.
Row 12 (WS): Kfb, k to 2 sts before m, k2tog, slm, k to m, slm, yo, k to 2 sts before m, k2tog. Leave marker on left needle. Turn to work RS.

Row 13 (RS): K to last st, yo, sl1 wyif.
Row 14 (WS): Kfb, k to 2 sts before m, k2tog, slm, k to m. Leave marker on left needle. Turn to work RS.

Row 15 (RS): K to last st, yo, sl1 wyif.
Row 16 (WS): Kfb, k to 2 sts before m, k2tog. Leave marker on left needle. Turn to work RS.

Row 17 (RS): K to last st, yo, sl1 wyif.
In the next row, close the short row gap after each "k2tog, slm" by picking up the garter stitch bump with left needle, slip the picked up stitch knit-wise with right needle, slip the next stitch knit-wise with right needle, k those 2 sts together tbl.

Row 18 (WS): Kfb, *k to 2 sts before m, k2tog, slm, close short row gap, k to m, slm, yo, repeat from * 3 more times, k to last 3 sts, k2tog, sl1 wyif.

Repeat Rows 1-18 once more. Break color C. Place all sts onto a spare circular needle or leave them on the needle and use a new circular needle for the next section.

SECTION 3

Place the last 10 sts from SECTION 1 onto a circular or double pointed needle. All remaining sts from SECTION 1 should be on another circular needle.

Use color B for the Small Size cabled edging. Use color D for the Large Size cabled edging if you wish to have a new color for the cable like the photographed sample (cable shown in variegated gray).

Row 1 (RS): Using color B [D], k10.
Row 2 (WS): P9, p2tog (last st together with next color B stitch). Turn to work RS.

Row 3 (RS): C10B.
Row 4 (WS): P9, p2tog (last st together with next color B stitch). Turn to work RS.

Row 5 (RS): K10.
Row 6 (WS): P9, p2tog (last st together with next color B stitch). Turn to work RS.

Repeat rows 5 & 6 3 more times.

Repeat Rows 3-12 until you run out of sts to attach the cable.

Using color C and with RS facing, pick up and k into selvedge starting at the corner near the live sts. (Pick up and k1 selvedge st, m1) 36 times for Small Size or 20 times for Large Size. Your needle tips should now be facing each other. Break color C.

Using color B [D], continue to work Rows 3-12 of the attached cable until all color C selvedge sts are joined to the cable.

Next Row (RS): K10.
Next Row (WS): Cast on 3 sts using the cable cast on method. *K2, k2tog tbl, repeat from * until all 10 color B [D] sts are bound off. Break yarn and place 3 sts onto waste yarn. You will use these 3 sts later.

I-cord Edge
This next row is worked across all the color C stitches on your needle. Use color B in the next row if you wish to add a color pop I-cord or use color C if you wish to bind off in the same border color.

Next Row (RS): K all sts. If you want a color-blocked I-cord edge, then knit a different color before each marker and leave the color attached so you can bind off on the next WS row.

Next Row (WS): Place 3 sts from cabled edge onto left needle. Using your chosen color for the I-cord bind off, *k2, k2tog tbl, repeat from * to end of row. If you are working a color-blocked I-cord edge, BO in color to m and then switch bind off colors after each marker.

Break yarn and pull it through the last 3 sts.

FINISHING

Weave in ends and block the finished scarf to smooth the fabric and exaggerate the jagged border.

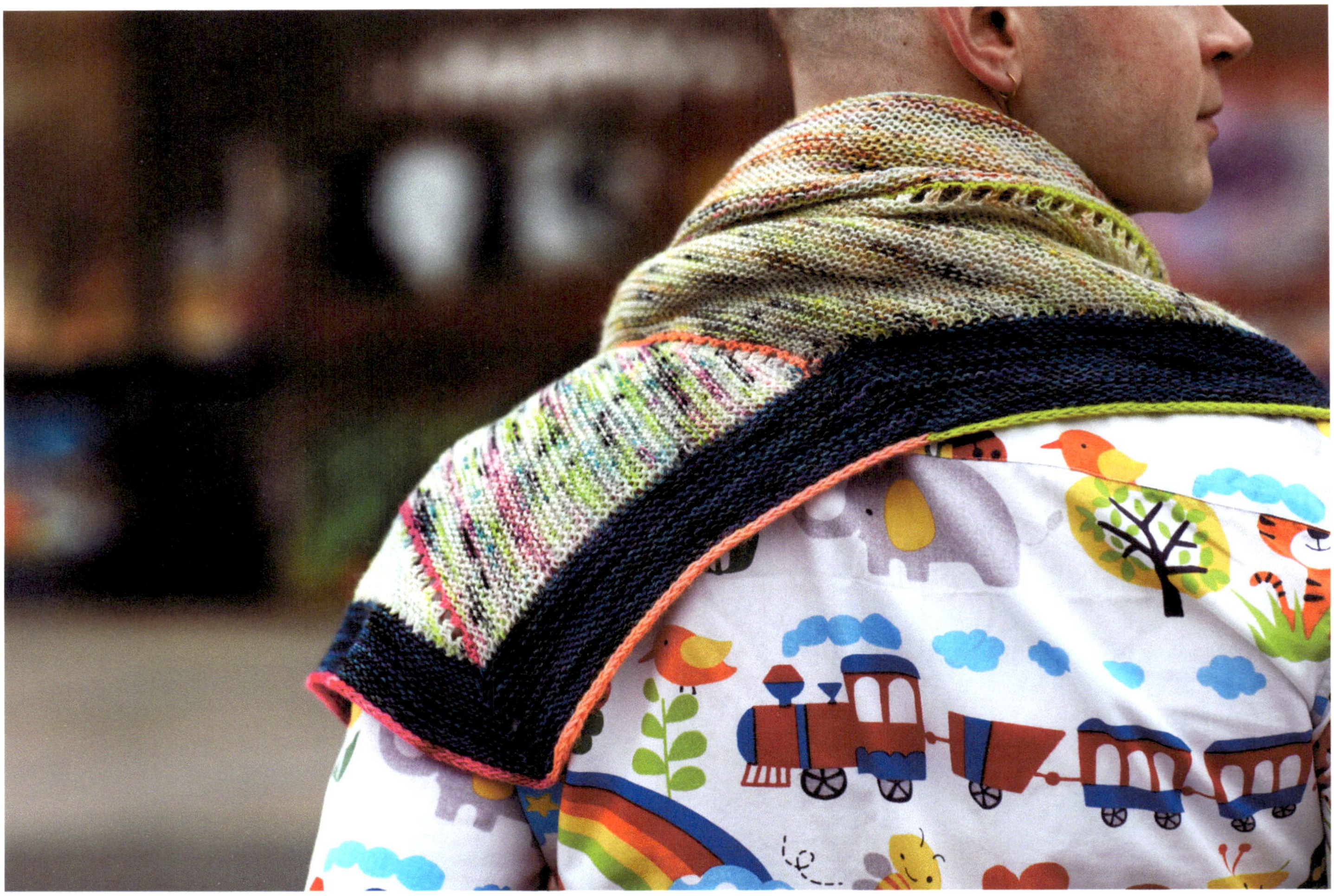

81

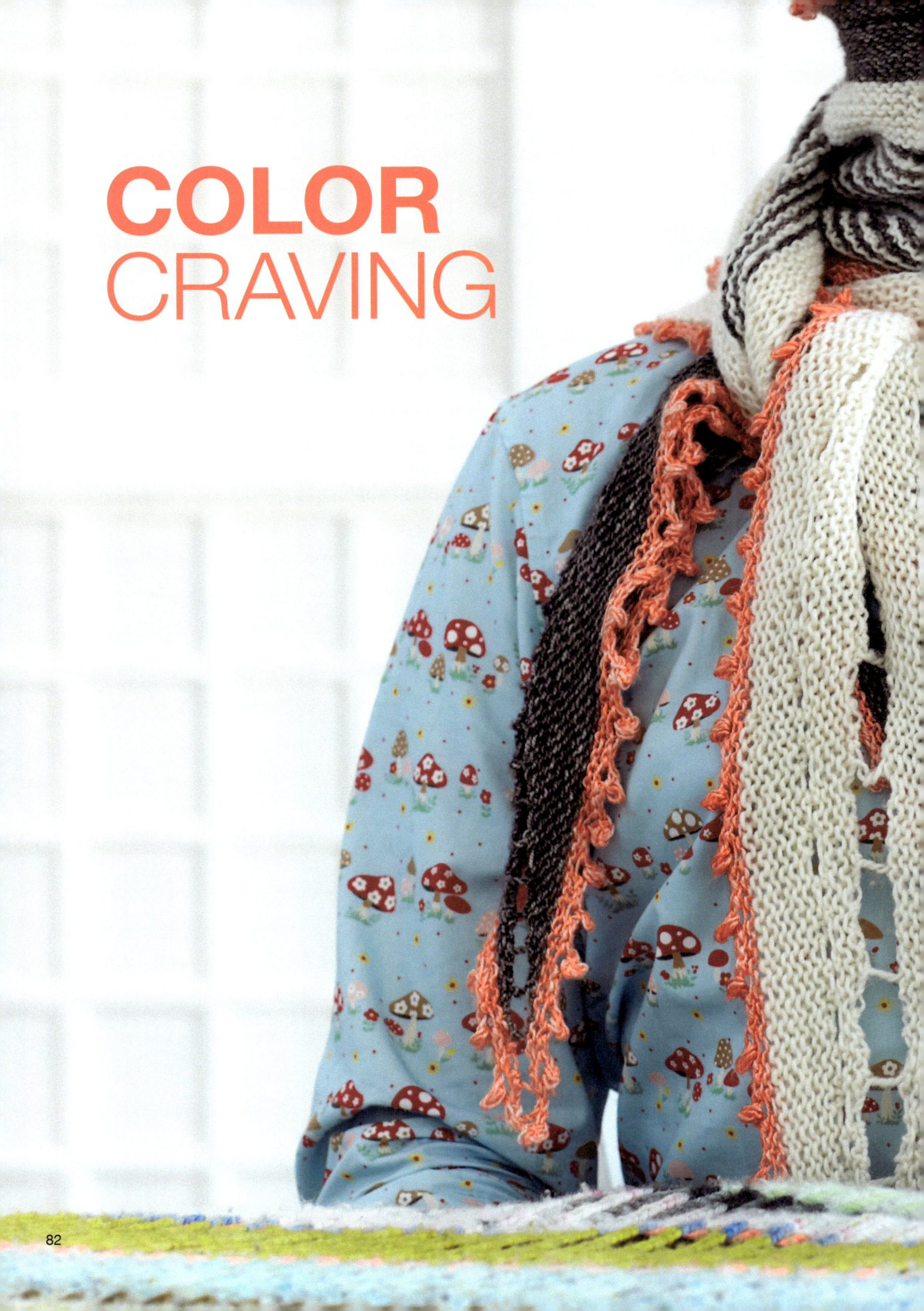

COLOR
CRAVING

83

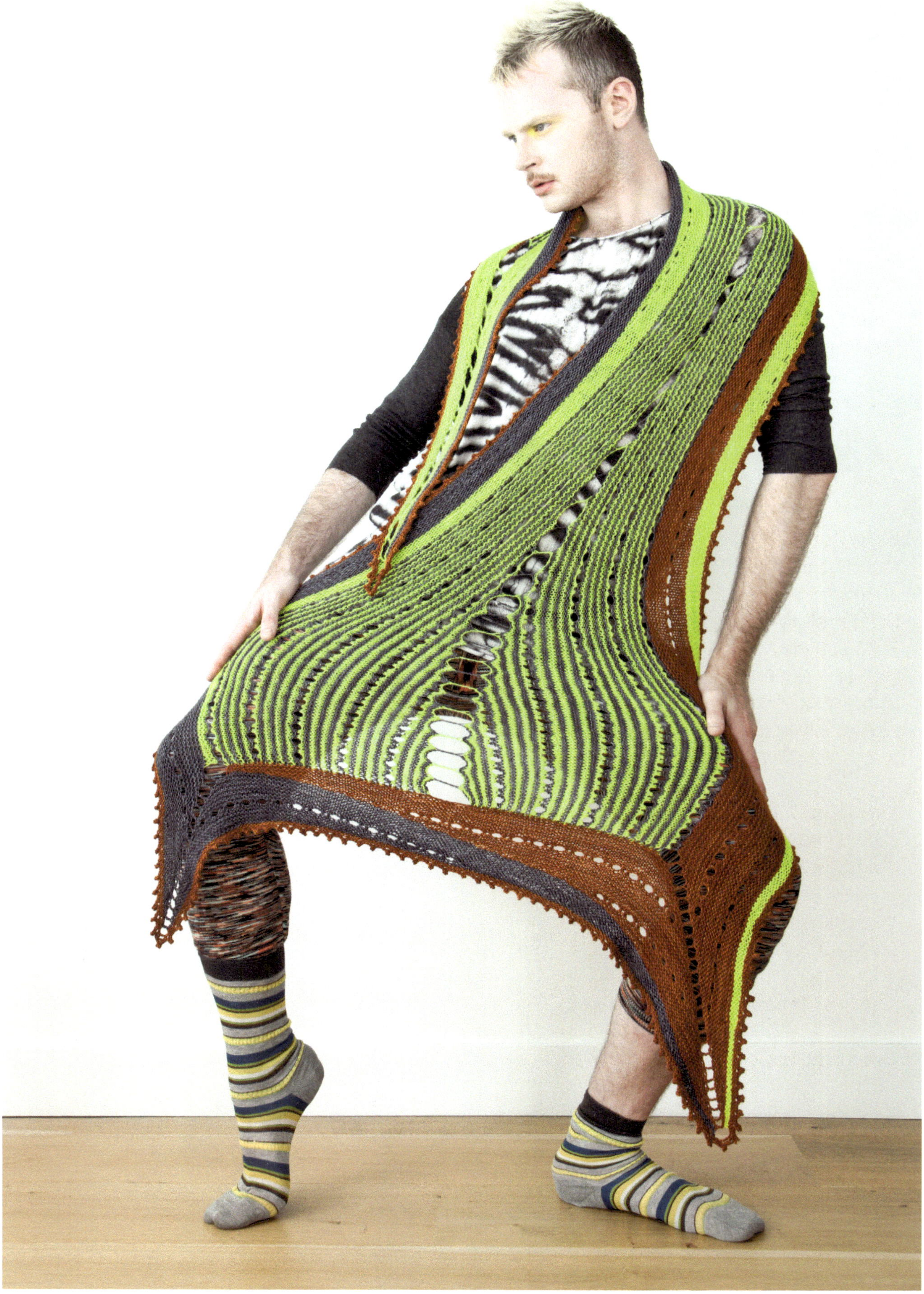

COLOR CRAVING

This long scarf begins with two stitches and quickly increases in size with five yarn overs every other row. The giant holes elongate the shape and three final short row wedges are added at each corner, producing bold color blocks.

Finished Measurements: 75" / 190cm long, 38" / 97cm at widest part.
Measurements taken after blocking.

Yarn: Fingering weight

Shown in: Green Version
The Plucky Knitter Primo Fingering
(75% Merino, 20% Cashmere, 5% Nylon; 390yds / 357m per 100g skein)
Color A - Lonesome Highway
Color B - Tiptoe
Color C - Sticky Toffee

Pink Version
Viola Merino Fingering (100% Merino; 400yds / 366m per 100g skein) Color A - Slate
Schoppel- Wolle Leinen Los (70% Wool, 30% Flax; 328yds / 300m per 100g ball)
Color B - 0980 White
Isager Strik Plant Fibre 2 (70% Cellulose, 15% Hemp, 15% Bamboo; 164yds / 150m per 50g ball) Color C - 64 Pink

Yardage: Color A - 340yds / 311m
Color B - 345yds / 315m
Color C - 300yds / 274m

Needles: 40" US 6 / 4mm circular
spare 40" circular needle same size or smaller.

Notions: Tapestry needle

Gauge: 20 sts & 48 rows = 4" / 10cm in garter stitch

Pattern Notes: Use these video tutorials to assist with Sections 1 & 2:
http://www.youtube.com/ watch?v=jjBsw9t3pXQ&feature=em-share_video_user

http://youtu.be/4cOdXveLGYI

STITCH COUNT CHART

Use this chart to help reassure your stitch counts as you reach the middle of each RS row.

The number in the left column is the RS row number.

The right column shows the number of stitches knit until you reach the middle of the row before executing "yo 5 times".

Row #	K to Middle of Row	Row #	K to Middle of Row
3	6	43	106
5	11	45	111
7	16	47	116
9	21	49	yo row
11	26	51	126
13	31	53	131
15	36	55	136
17	yo row	57	141
19	46	59	146
21	51	61	151
23	56	63	156
25	61	65	yo row
27	66	67	166
29	71	69	171
31	76	71	176
33	yo row	73	181
35	86	75	186
37	91	77	191
39	96	79	196
41	101	81	yo row

INSTRUCTIONS
SECTION 1

Using A, CO 2 sts. (Instead of doing a slip knot followed by one long tail CO stitch, just place the strand of yarn on top of the needle and then work 1 long tail CO stitch).

Row 1 (RS): K1, yo 5 times, sl1 wyif.
Row 2 (WS): K1, k1/p1 into each yo (10 total sts), sl1 wyif.

Row 3 (RS): Using B, k to middle of row, yo 5 times, k to last st, sl1 wyif.
Row 4 (WS): K to 5 yo's, k1/p1 into each yo (10 total sts), k to last st, sl1 wyif.

Row 5 (RS): Using A, k to middle of row, yo 5 times, k to last st, sl1 wyif.
Row 6 (WS): K to 5 yo's, k1/p1 into each yo (10 total sts), k to last st, sl1 wyif.

Repeat last 4 Rows twice more, then repeat Rows 3 & 4 once more. 82 sts. Carry colors A & B along the right edge as you stripe colors. As you knit a few stripes, the 2-stitch CO will look a little loose and messy. You can pull on the yarn from the CO to undo it, leaving a gap.

Row 17 (RS): Using A, k1, (k2tog, yo twice, ssk) 10 times, yo 5 times, (k2tog, yo twice, ssk) 10 times, sl1 wyif.
Row 18 (WS): K1, (k1, k1/p1 into double yo, k1) 10 times, k1/p1 into each of the 5 yo's (10 total sts), (k1, k1/p1 into double yo, k1) 10 times, sl1 wyif. 92 sts.

Repeat Rows 3-6 three more times, then repeat Rows 3 & 4 once more. 162 sts.

Row 33 (RS): Using A, k1, (k2tog, yo twice, ssk) 20 times, yo 5 times, (k2tog, yo twice, ssk) 20 times, sl1 wyif.
Row 34 (WS): K1, (k1, k1/p1 into double yo, k1) 20 times, k1/p1 into each of the 5 yo's (10 total sts), (k1, k1/p1 into double yo, k1) 20 times, sl1 wyif. 172 sts.

Repeat Rows 3-6 three more times, then repeat Rows 3 & 4 once more. 242 sts.

Row 49 (RS): Using A, k1 (k2tog, yo twice, ssk) 30 times, yo 5 times, (k2tog, yo twice, ssk) 30 times, sl1 wyif.
Row 50 (WS): K1, (k1, k1/p1 into double yo, k1) 30 times, k1/p1 into each of the 5 yo's (10 total sts), (k1, k1/p1 into double yo, k1) 30 times, sl1 wyif. 252 sts.

Repeat Rows 3-6 three more times, then repeat Rows 3 & 4 once more. 322 sts.

Row 65 (RS): Using A, k1 (k2tog, yo twice, ssk) 40 times, yo 5 times, (k2tog, yo twice, ssk) 40 times, sl1 wyif.
Row 66 (WS): K1, (k1, k1/p1 into double yo, k1) 40 times, k1/p1 into each of the 5 yo's (10 total sts), (k1, k1/p1 into double yo, k1) 40 times, sl1 wyif. 332 sts.

87

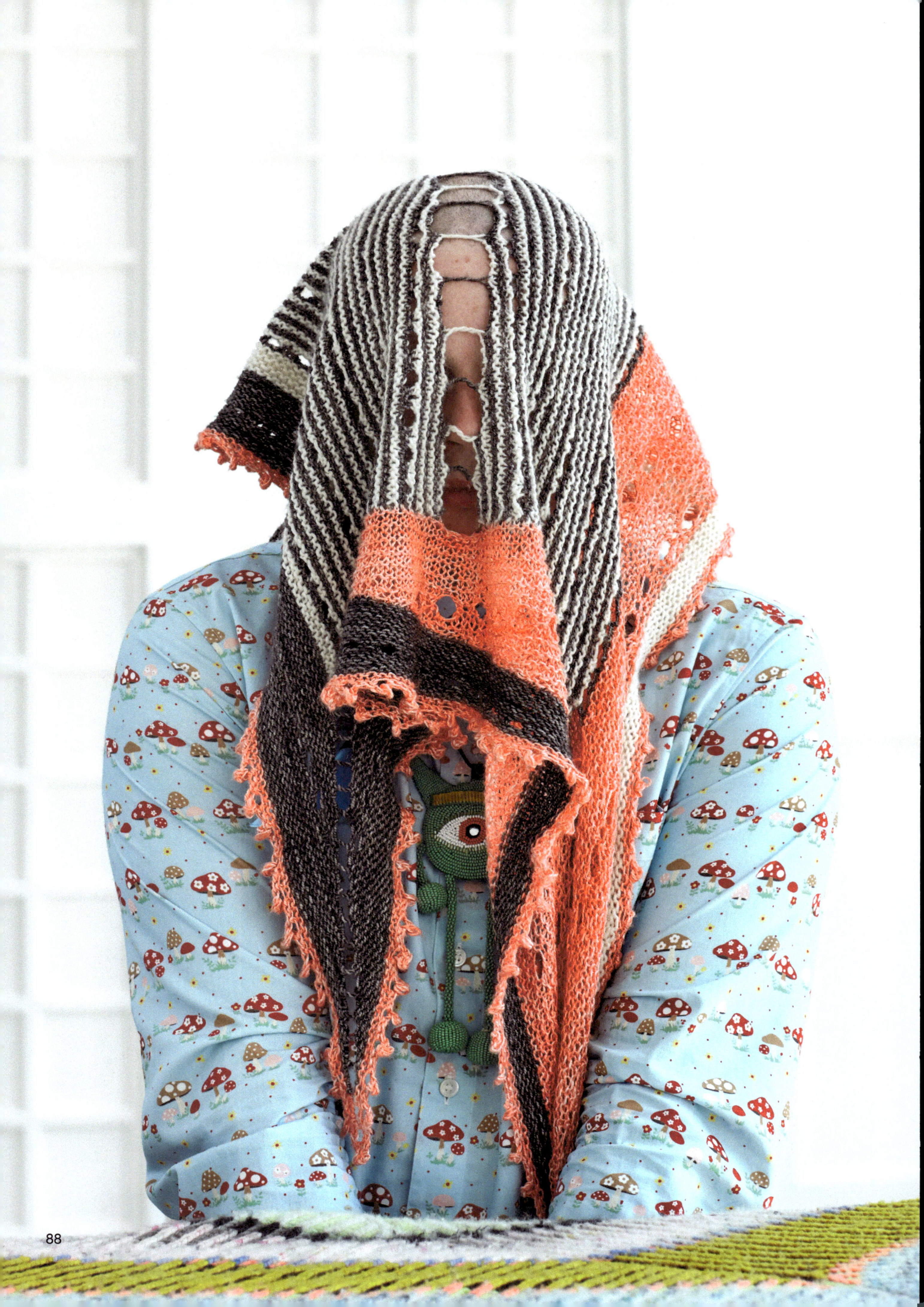

Repeat Rows 3-6 three more times, then repeat Rows 3 & 4 once more. 402 sts.

Row 81 (RS): Using A, k1 (k2tog, yo twice, ssk) 50 times, yo 5 times, (k2tog, yo twice, ssk) 50 times, sl1 wyif.
Row 82 (WS): K1, (k1, k1/p1 into double yo, k1) 50 times, k1/p1 into each of the 5 yo's (10 total sts), (k1, k1/p1 into double yo, k1) 50 times, sl1 wyif. 412 sts. Break colors A & B.

SECTION 2
Row 1 (RS): Using C and with RS facing, pick up and k39 sts along SECTION 1 selvedge (1 picked up stitch into each selvedge stitch starting at the corner next to the last live stitch from SECTION 1), CO 5 sts using the cable CO method, pick up and k39 sts (1 picked up stitch into each selvedge stitch), k1, yo twice, k204, sl1 wyif. Slip remaining 206 sts from the left half of SECTION 1 onto a spare circular needle.
Row 2 (WS): K to double yo, k1/p1 into each yo (4 total sts), k to last st, sl1 wyif.

Row 3 (RS): K86, yo twice, k to 11 sts before end of row, turn to work WS.
Row 4 (WS): K to double yo, k1/p1 into each yo (4 total sts), k to 5 sts before end of row, turn to work RS.

Row 5 (RS): K to middle of yo hole, yo twice, k to 11 sts before last turn, turn to work WS.
Row 6 (WS): K to double yo, k1/p1 into each yo (4 total sts), k to 5 sts before last turn, turn to work RS.

Repeat last 2 rows 4 more times.

Row 15 (RS): K5, (k2tog, yo twice, ssk) 15 times, k3, yo twice, k3, (k2tog, yo twice, ssk) 34 times, k3, turn to work WS.
Row 16 (WS): K3, (k1, k1/p1 into double yo, k1) 34 times, k3, k1/p1 into each yo (4 total sts), k3, (k1, k1/p1 into double yo, k1) 15 times, turn to work RS.

Repeat Rows 5 & 6 seven more times.

Row 31 (RS): K5, (k2tog, yo twice, ssk) 9 times, k3, yo twice, k3, (k2tog, yo twice, ssk) 16 times, k3, turn to work WS.
Row 32 (WS): K3, (k1, k1/p1 into double yo, k1) 16 times, k3, k1/p1 into each yo (4 total sts), k3, (k1, k1/p1 into double yo, k1) 9 times, turn to work RS.

Repeat Rows 5 & 6 seven more times.

Row 47 (RS): K to middle of yo hole, yo twice, k to last color C st (closing the short row gaps), sl1 wyif.
Row 48 (WS): K to double yo, k1/p1 into each yo (4 total sts), k to last color C st (closing the short row gaps), sl1 wyif.

There should be 385 total color C sts. Break color C.

SECTION 3
This section uses the same techniques as SECTION 2, but with different numbers and color B. You can refer back to the Clue 2 video (http://youtu.be/4cOdXveLGYI) for the yarn over and short row technique demonstrations.

With RS facing, slip 132 color C sts onto a spare circular needle. You should now be at the middle of the color C yo hole.

Row 1 (RS): Using color B, k the remaining 253 C sts (you should now be at the gap between color C and color A), yo 5 times, k205 sts from spare circular needle (the live color A sts from SECTION 1), sl1 wyif (the last color A st).
Row 2 (WS): K to 5 yo's, k1/p1 into each yo (10 total sts), k to last color B st, sl1 wyif. 469 sts.

Row 3 (RS): K to middle of yo hole, yo 5 times, k to 19 sts before end of row, turn to work WS.
Row 4 (WS): K to 5 yo's, k1/p1 into each yo (10 total sts), k to 22 sts before end of row, turn to work RS.

Row 5(RS): K to middle of yo hole, yo 5 times, k to 19 sts before last turn, turn to work WS.
Row 6 (WS): K to 5 yo's, k1/p1 into each yo (10 total sts), k to 22 sts before last turn, turn to work RS.

Repeat last 2 rows 4 more times.

Row 15 (RS): K22, (k2tog, yo twice, ssk) 33 times, k2, yo 5 times, k2, (k2tog, yo twice, ssk) 26 times, k2, turn to work WS.
Row 16 (WS): K2, (k1, k1 into first yo, p1 into second yo, k1) 26 times, k2, k1/p1 into each yo (10 total sts), k2, (k1, k1 into first yo, p1 into second yo, k1) 33 times, turn to work RS.

Repeat Rows 5 & 6 seven more times.

Row 31 (RS): K to middle of yo hole, yo 5 times, k to last color B st (closing the short Row gaps), sl1 wyif.
Row 32 (WS): K to 5 yo's, k1/p1 into each yo (10 total sts), k to last color B st (closing the short row gaps), sl1 wyif. There should be 619 total color B sts. Break color B.

SECTION 4
With RS facing, slip 333 color B sts onto spare circular needle (all sts until reaching the middle of the 5 yo hole).

Row 1 (RS): Using A, k the remaining 286 B sts, yo twice, k131 sts from spare circular needle (the live color C sts from SECTION 2), sl1 wyif.
Row 2 (WS): K to double yo, k1/p1 into each yo (4 total sts), k to last st, sl1 wyif. 422 sts.

Row 3 (RS): K to middle of yo hole, yo twice, k to 10 sts before end of row, turn to work WS.
Row 4 (WS): K to double yo, k1/p1 into each yo (4 total sts), k to 21 sts before end of row, turn to work RS.

Row 5(RS): K to middle of yo hole, yo twice, k to 10 sts before last turn, turn to work WS.
Row 6 (WS): K to double yo, k1/p1 into each yo (4 total sts), k to 21 sts before last turn, turn to work RS.

Repeat last 2 rows 4 more times.

Row 15 (RS): K21, (k2tog, yo twice, ssk) 38 times, k1, yo twice, k1, (k2tog, yo twice, ssk) 18 times, k3, turn to work WS.
Row 16 (WS): K3, (k1, k1/p1 into double yo, k1) 18 times, k1, k1/p1 into each yo (4 total sts), k1, (k1, k1/p1 into double yo, k1) 38 times, turn to work RS.

Repeat Rows 5 & 6 seven more times.

Row 31 (RS): K to middle of yo hole, yo twice, k to last color A st (closing the short row gaps), sl1 wyif.
Row 32 (WS): K to double yo, k1/p1 into each yo (4 total sts), k to last color A st (closing the short row gaps), sl1 wyif. Break color A. Turn to work RS.

BORDER
Rnd 1: Using C, *K to middle of yo hole, yo twice, repeat from * once more, k to end of color B (all B sts from spare circular needle), yo 5 times. Join to work in the rnd.
Rnd 2: *P to double yo, k1/p1 into each yo (4 total sts), repeat from * once more, p to 5 yo's, k1/p1 into each yo (10 total sts).
Rnd 3: *K to middle of yo hole, yo twice, repeat from * once more, k to middle of yo hole, yo 5 times, k5.
Rnd 4: *P to double yo, k1/p1 into each yo (4 total sts), repeat from * once more, p to 5 yo's, k1/p1 into each yo (10 total sts), p5.

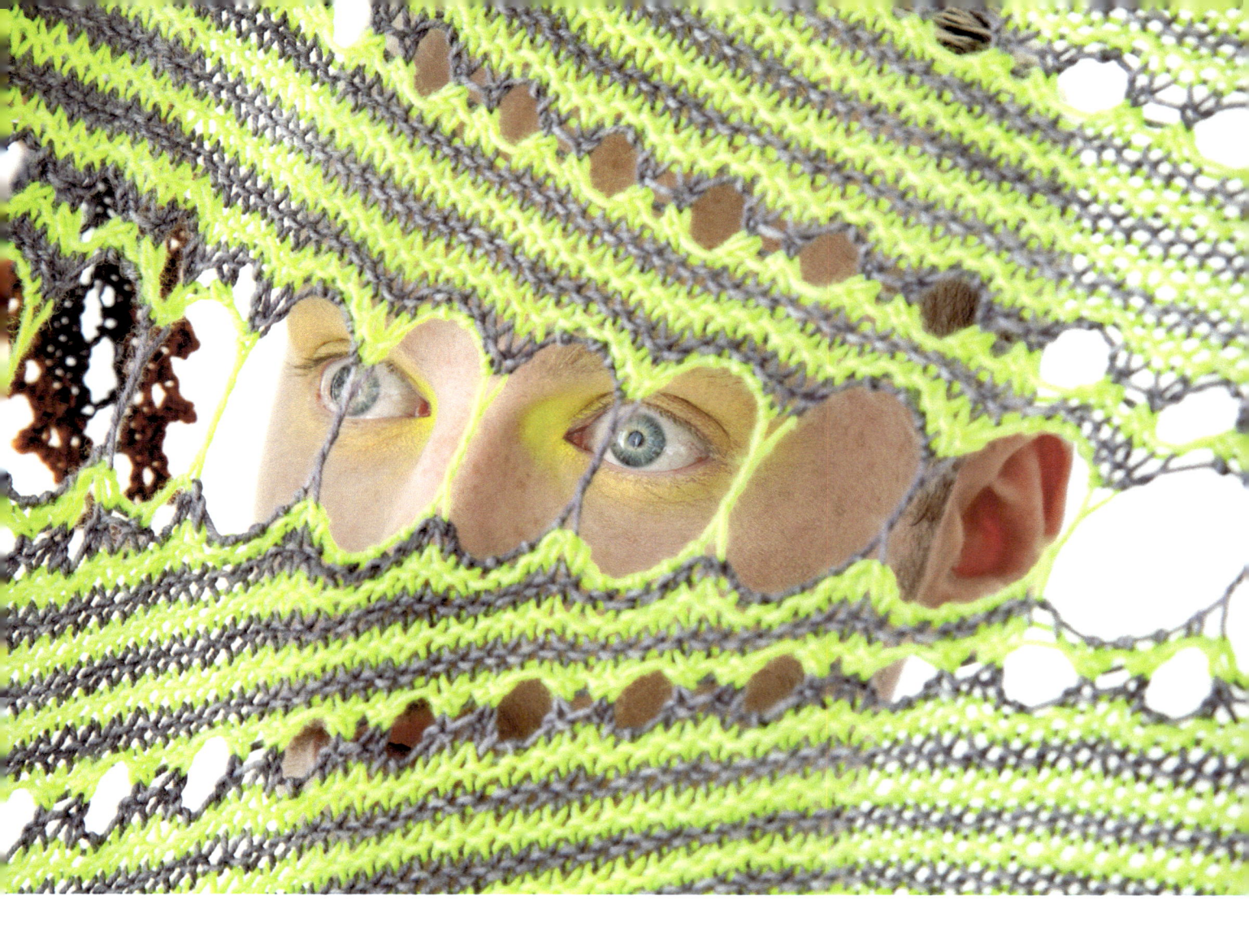

FINISHING

I recommend the picot BO for a flexible and decorative edge. The yardage estimates for this pattern reflect using the picot bind off. If you prefer an I-cord BO, that will require more yardage. Another BO option is the K2tog tbl BO. It will use less than the recommended yardage.

Picot BO

BO all sts with a picot BO as follows, *CO 3 sts using the cable CO method, BO 6 sts using the k2tog tbl BO method, repeat from * to end of rnd.

I-cord BO

If you prefer a more stream-lined finish to the shawl try working an I-cord BO as follows, CO 3 sts using the cable CO method, *k2, k2tog tbl, slip 3 sts back onto left needle, repeat from * to end of rnd. This BO will take more than the recommended yardage. You could also try working the BO in a fourth color.

K2tog tbl BO

For a quick and simple shawl edge, BO all sts as follows, *k2tog tbl, slip stitch back onto left needle, repeat from * to end of rnd.

Break yarn, weave in ends, block the finished shawl, and wear it with pride and joy!

ASKEWS ME
SHAWL

93

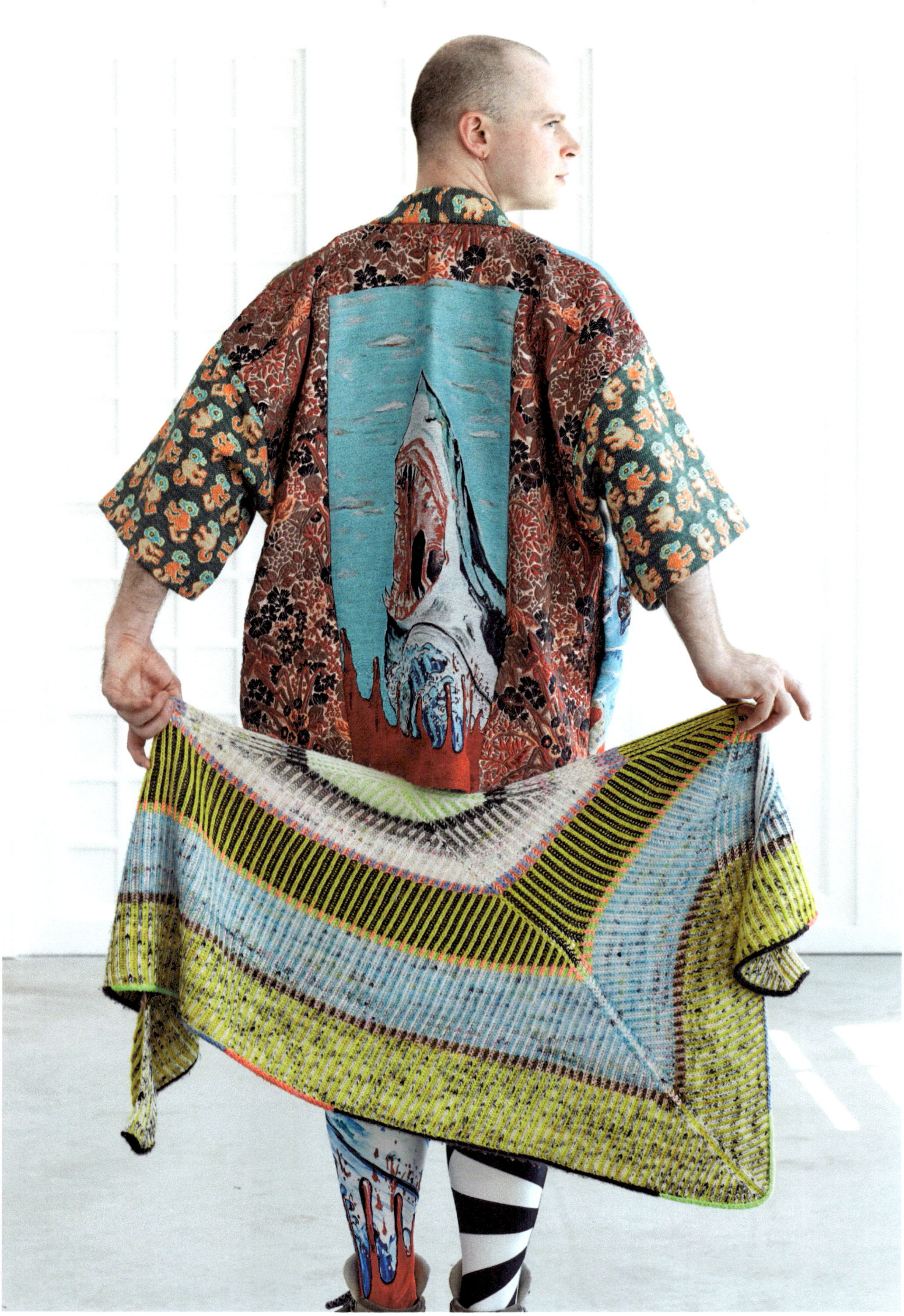

ASKEWS ME SHAWL

This top-down shawl is knit in two-color brioche stitch. The asymmetrical shape features half of a chevron that slants the ribbing to one side. Choose two colors or decorate the fabric with more colorful stripes.

Finished Measurements: 78" / 198cm wingspan length, 30" / 76cm along center spine. Measurements taken after blocking.

Yarn: Sport or DK weight

Shown in: Black & White Version
Malabrigo Arroyo (100% Superwash Merino; 335yds / 306m per 100g skein)
DC - Black
LC - Natural

Multi-color Version
Hedgehog Fibres Merino DK
Colors: Bike Bell, Where's My Bike?, Budgie, & Ferrum

Madelinetosh Tosh Sport
Colors: Optic, Oak, & Neon Peach

Woolfolk Får
Colors: Black, White

Madelinetosh DK Twist
Colors: Edison Bulb, Push Pop, Neon Lime

For a multi-color version, change yarn colors as you wish throughout the project. Remember, more is more and less is a bore.

Yardage: DC - 600yds / 549m
LC - 500yds / 457m

Needles: 40" US 6 / 4mm circular

Notions: 4 stitch markers, tapestry needle

Gauge: 16 sts & 26 rows = 4" / 10cm in two-color brioche stitch

Pattern Notes: In two-color brioche stitch, two rows are worked for each counted row that appears on the face of the fabric. The first color is worked across the row and then the row is worked again using the second color. The next row is worked the same way, once across with the first color and worked again with the second color. When counting rows, count only the stitches going up on a knit column. For example, when you work 4 rows, count 4 knit column stitches, even though you will have worked 8 rows back and forth. Two worked rows = One counted row.

When you put down your knitting and forget which color you just used and which color to use next, look at the color of the yo in the row just worked. That is the last color you used.

This shawl is written using a dark color (DC) and light color (LC) in the instructions. The RS features the DC and the WS features the LC.

INSTRUCTIONS

CO 9 sts loosely (with loose tension or with a needle that is a few sizes larger than the main needle) using the Two-Color CO.

Two-Color CO
Tie a slip knot in the dark color (DC) and slide the slip knot onto the left-hand needle.

Step 1: Knit into the DC slip knot with light color (LC), leaving the stitch on the left needle. Place the new stitch onto left needle, by slipping it knit-wise.
Step 2: Bring DC from behind and knit into gap between last two stitches on left needle with DC (like a cable CO)
Step 3: Place new knitted stitch onto left needle by slipping it knit-wise. Repeat from step 2 alternating LC & DC stitch until 9 sts are cast on. The first and last stitch should be with DC.

Set-Up Row 1 RS DC: (K1, sl1yo) 4 times, k1. Do not turn, slide stitches to work the same row with the other color.
Set-Up Row 1 RS LC: LC is hanging in back, sl1, yf, (brp1, sl1yo) 3 times, brp1, drop LC to front, sl last st. Turn work.

Set-Up Row 2 WS DC: P1, sl1yo, (brp1, sl1yo) 3 times, p1. Do not turn, slide stitches to work the same row with the other color.
Set-Up Row 2 WS LC: LC is hanging in back, sl1, (brk1, sl1yo) 3 times, brk1, drop LC to back, sl last st. Turn work.

Set-Up Row 3 RS DC: K1, sl1 yo, (brk1, sl1yo) 3 times, k1. Do not turn, slide stitches to work the same row with the other color.
Set-Up Row 3 RS LC: LC is hanging in front, sl1, (brp1, sl1yo) 3 times, brp1, drop LC to front, sl last st. Turn work.

Set-Up Row 4 WS DC: P1, sl1yo, (brp1, sl1yo) 3 times, p1. Do not turn, slide stitches to work the same row with the other color.
Set-Up Row 4 WS LC: LC is hanging in back, sl1, (brk1, sl1yo) 3 times, brk1, drop LC to back, sl last st. Turn work.

Repeat Row 3 with DC once more. Do not turn work. Instead, rotate rectangle to look at the DC selvedge. Using DC, pick up and k3 sts along DC selvedge. Rotate again to pick up and k9 sts along CO edge. 21 sts. Do not turn work. Slide stitches to work the RS with LC.

Next Row RS LC: LC is hanging in front, sl1, yf, (brp1, sl1yo) 4 times, (p1, sl1yo) 5 times, p1, drop LC to front, sl last st. Turn to work WS.

Next Row WS DC: P1, sl1yo, (brp1, sl1yo) 9 times, p1. Do not turn, slide stitches to work the same row with the other color.
Next Row WS LC: LC is hanging in back, sl1, (brk1, sl1yo) 9 times, brk1, drop LC to back, sl last st. Turn work.

Next Row RS DC: K1, sl1 yo, (brk1, sl1yo) 3 times, pm, brkyobrk, sl1yo, brkyobrk, pm, sl1yo, brkyobrk, pm, (sl1yo, brk1) 3 times, sl1yo, k1. Do not turn, slide stitches to work the same row with the other color. 27 sts. In the following rows, slip the stitch markers as you come to them.
Next Row RS LC: LC is hanging in front, sl1, (brp1, sl1yo) to last 2 sts, brp1, drop LC to front, sl last st. Turn work.

Next Row WS DC: P1, sl1yo, (brp1, sl1yo) to last st, p1. Do not turn, slide stitches to work the same row with the other color.
Next Row WS LC: LC is hanging in back, sl1, brk1, (sl1yo, brk1) to last st, drop LC to back, sl last st. Turn work.

97

98

SECTION 1

Row 1 RS DC: K1, sl1 yo, (brk1, sl1yo) 3 times, slm, brkyobrk, sl1yo, (brk1, sl1yo) to 1 st before m, brkyobrk, slm, sl1yo, (brk1, sl1yo) to 1 st before m, brkyobrk, slm, (sl1yo, brk1) 3 times, sl1yo, k1. Do not turn, slide stitches to work the same row with the other color. In the next RS row with LC the yo st from each brkyobrk will just be a p1 instead of a brp1 since that stitch is so fresh without its yo.

Row 1 RS LC: LC is hanging in front, sl1, (brp1, sl1yo) to last 2 sts, brp1, drop LC to front, sl last st. Turn work.

Row 2 WS DC: P1, sl1yo, (brp1, sl1yo) to last st, p1. Do not turn, slide stitches to work the same row with the other color.

Row 2 WS LC: LC is hanging in back, sl1, brk1, (sl1yo, brk1) to last st, drop LC to back, sl last st. Turn work.

Repeat Rows 1 & 2 with DC & LC 24 more times. 177 sts.

SECTION 2

Row 1 RS DC: K1, sl1 yo, (brk1, sl1yo) 3 times, slm, brkyobrk, sl1yo, (brk1, sl1yo) to 1 st before m, brkyobrk, slm, sl1yo, pm, brkyobrk, sl1yo, (brk1, sl1yo) 23 times, brRsl dec, pm, sl1yo, brkyobrk, slm, (sl1yo, brk1) 3 times, sl1yo, k1. Do not turn, slide stitches to work the same row with the other color.

Row 1 RS LC: LC is hanging in front, sl1, (brp1, sl1yo) to last 2 sts, brp1, drop LC to front, sl last st. Turn work.

Row 2 WS DC: P1, sl1yo, (brp1, sl1yo) to last st, p1. Do not turn, slide stitches to work the same row with the other color.

Row 2 WS LC: LC is hanging in back, sl1, brk1, (sl1yo, brk1) to last st, drop LC to back, sl last st. Turn work.

Row 3 RS DC: K1, sl1 yo, (brk1, sl1yo) 3 times, slm, brkyobrk, sl1yo, (brk1, sl1yo) to 1 st before m, brkyobrk, slm, sl1yo, slm, brkyobrk, sl1yo, (brk1, sl1yo) 23 times, brRsl dec, slm, sl1yo, (brk1, sl1yo) to 1 st before m, brkyobrk, slm, (sl1yo, brk1) 3 times, sl1yo, k1. Do not turn, slide stitches to work the same row with the other color.
Row 3 RS LC: LC is hanging in front, sl1, (brp1, sl1yo) to last 2 sts, brp1, drop LC to front, sl last st. Turn work.

Row 4 WS DC: P1, sl1yo, (brp1, sl1yo) to last st, p1. Do not turn, slide stitches to work the same row with the other color.
Row 4 WS LC: LC is hanging in back, sl1, brk1, (sl1yo, brk1) to last st, drop LC to back, sl last st. Turn work.

Repeat Rows 3 & 4 with DC & LC 32 more times or until shawl reach desired length ending with Row 4 WS LC. 381 sts. Break LC.

Next Row RS DC: K2, (brk1, k1) 3 times, slm, brkyobrk, k1, (brk1, k1) to 1 st before m, brkyobrk, slm, k1, slm, brkyobrk, k1, (brk1, k1) 23 times, brRsl dec, slm, k1, (brk1, k1) to 1 st before m, brkyobrk, slm, (k1, brk1) 3 times, k2. Turn work to BO sts on WS.

FINISHING
BO all sts on the WS row with DC as follows, CO 3 sts using the cable CO method, *k2, k2tog tbl, slip 3 sts onto left needle, repeat from * until all sts are bound off. Break yarn and pull it through the remaining 3 sts. Weave in ends and block finished shawl.

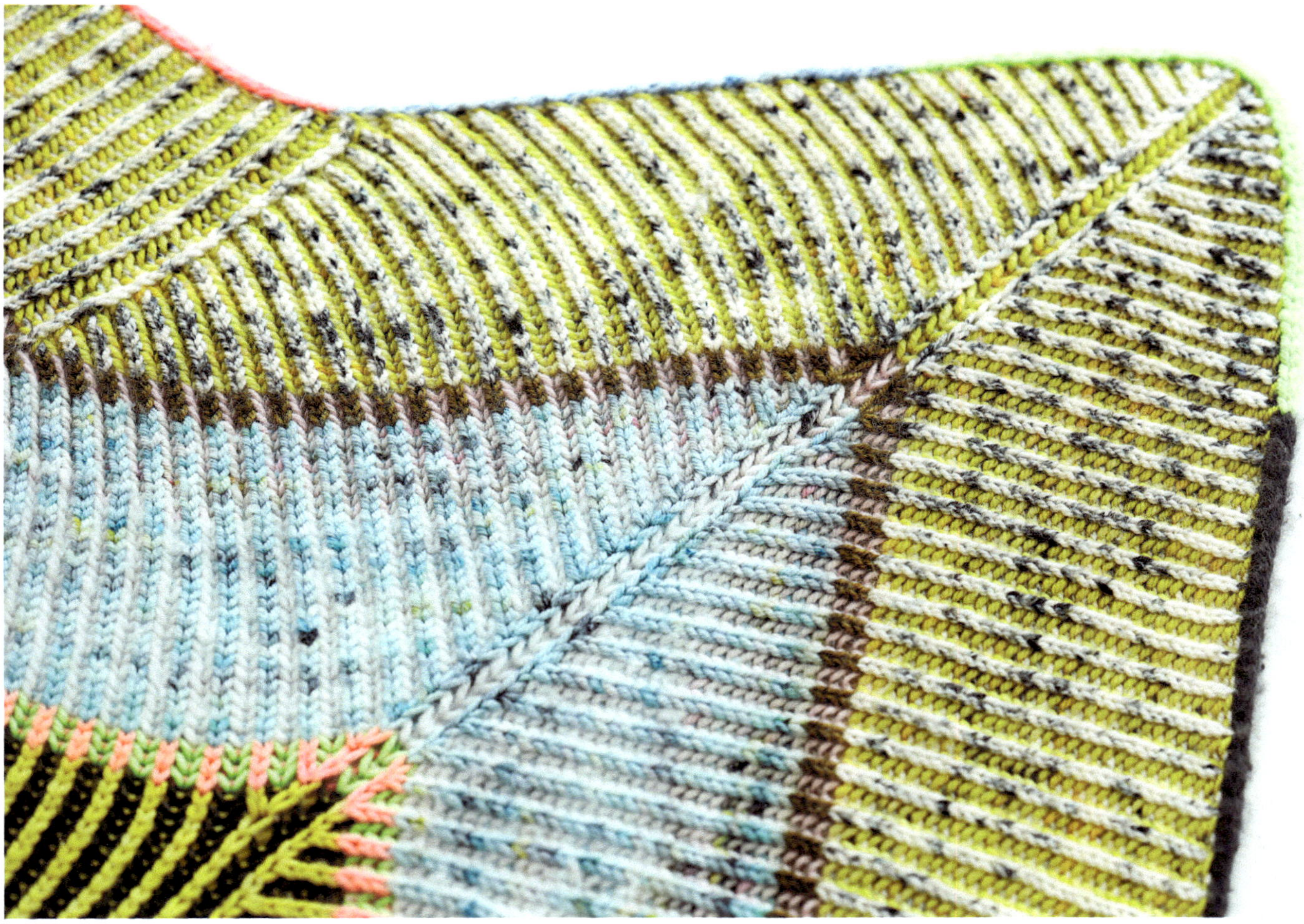

102

KNIT 'N SLIDE

Small Size
3 colors

KNIT 'N SLIDE

This top-down shawl is shaped with yarn overs for a long semi-circle shape. The first section uses the knit 'n slide technique, a super easy trick that creates the illusion of 2 rows knit/2 rows purl texture, but you're only knitting! The lacy border features a contrast color and giant yarn over wraps with Westknits shortcut rows to create the large scallops.

Sizes: Small (Large)

Finished Measurements: 86 [96]" / 218 [244] cm wingspan length, 20 [24]" / 51 [61]cm from CO to BO. Measurements taken after blocking.

Yarn: Fingering weight.
Large size uses a lace weight mohair/silk for the border.

Shown in: Small Size (3 colors)
Hedgehog Fibres Sock Yarn (85% Merino, 15% Nylon; 437yds / 400m per 100g skein)
Color A - Graphite
Color B - Crystal
Color C - Budgie

Large Size (4 colors)
Hedgehog Fibres Sock Yarn (85% Merino, 15% Nylon; 437yds / 400m per 100g skein)
Color A - Night Ride
Color B - Oh Snap!
Color D - High Kick

Hedgehog Fibres Kidsilk Lace (70% Mohair, 30% Silk; 459yds / 420m per 50g skein)
Color C - Highlighter

Yardage: Small Size
Color A (dark gray) - 430yds / 393m
Color B (light gray) - 280 / 256m
Color C (blue) - 200yds / 183m

Large Size
Color A - 325yds / 297m
Color B - 325 yds / 297m
Color C (mohair) - 250yds / 229m
Color D (border speckle) - 300yds / 274m

Needles: 60" US 4 / 3.5mm circular

Notions: Tapestry needle

Gauge: 22 sts & 42 rows = 4" / 10cm in Knit 'n Slide pattern

Pattern Notes: Carry colors A & B along the edge while striping colors.

Knit 'n Slide: Each color is worked for 1 row in Section 1. First, knit the row with color A, then slide all the stitches to the other needle and work that same side with color B. Then turn and knit the other side with color A followed by knitting that side again with color B. Circular needles are necessary so the stitches slide to the other needle tip like a typewriter.

Colors A & B are used for 1-row stripes. The sample colors in the large speckled size (Night Ride & Oh Snap!) create a beautiful blended effect because they share similar colors. If you have 2 high contrast colors for A & B you will get a striped effect like the smaller gray sample.

INSTRUCTIONS
SECTION 1

Using A, CO 3 sts. K7 rows.
At the end of last row, do not turn to work other side, rotate piece 90 degrees clockwise so that you are looking at the long side of the garter rectangle. Pick up and k3 sts in the purl bump of each garter ridge. Rotate piece another 90 degrees. Pick up and k3 sts along the CO edge. 9 sts. Turn to work WS row.

Set Up Row (WS): K3, yo, k3, yo, k3. 11 sts. Slide sts to work the WS row again.
Set Up Row (WS): Using B, k3, yo, k5, yo, k3. 13 sts. Turn to work RS.

Row 1 (RS): Using A, k3, (yo, k1) 7 times, yo, k3. 21 sts. Slide sts to work the RS row again.
Row 2 (RS): Using B, k3, yo, k to last 3 sts, yo, k3. 23 sts. Turn to work WS.

Row 3 (WS): Using A, k3, yo, k to last 3 sts, yo, k3. 25 sts. Slide sts to work the WS row again.
Row 4 (WS): Using B, k3, yo, k to last 3 sts, yo, k3. 27 sts. Turn to work RS.

> **Row 5 (RS):** Using A, k3, yo, k to last 3 sts, yo, k3. Slide sts to work the RS row again.
> **Row 6 (RS):** Using B, k3, yo, k to last 3 sts, yo, k3. Turn to work WS.
> **Row 7 (WS):** Using A, k3, yo, k to last 3 sts, yo, k3. Slide sts to work the WS row again.
> **Row 8 (WS):** Using B, k3, yo, k to last 3 sts, yo, k3. Turn to work RS.

Repeat last 4 rows 2 more times. 51 sts.

Row 17 (RS): Using A, k3, (yo, k1, yo, k2tog) 15 times, yo, k3. 67 sts. Slide sts to work the RS row again.
Row 18 (RS): Using B, k3, yo, k to last 3 sts, yo, k3. 69 sts. Turn to work WS.

Row 19 (WS): Using A, k3, yo, k to last 3 sts, yo, k3. 71 sts. Slide sts to work the WS row again.
Row 20 (WS): Using B, k3, yo, k to last 3 sts, yo, k3. 73 sts. Turn to work RS.

Repeat Rows 5-8 6 times. 121 sts.

Row 45 (RS): Using A, k3, (yo, k1, yo, k2tog) to last 4 sts, k1, yo, k3. 160 sts. Slide sts to work the RS row again.
Row 46 (RS): Using B, k3, yo, k to last 3 sts, yo, k3. 162 sts. Turn to work WS.

Row 47 (WS): Using A, k3, yo, k to last 3 sts, yo, k3. 164 sts. Slide sts to work the WS row again.
Row 48 (WS): Using B, k3, yo, k to last 3 sts, yo, k3. 166 sts. Turn to work RS.

Repeat Rows 5-8 10 times. 246 sts.

Row 89 (RS): Using A, k3, (yo, k1, yo, k2tog) to last 3 sts, yo, k3. 327 sts. Slide sts to work the RS row again.
Row 90 (RS): Using B, k3, yo, k to last 3 sts, yo, k3. 329 sts. Turn to work WS.

Row 91 (WS): Using A, k3, yo, k to last 3 sts, yo, k3. 331 sts. Slide sts to work the WS row again.
Row 92 (WS): Using B, k3, yo, k to last 3 sts, yo, k3. 333 sts. Turn to work RS.

Repeat Rows 5-8 10 [15] times. 413 [453] sts. Skip to SECTION 2 for Small Size. Continue with Stripes for Large Size.

Stripes - Large Size Only
The following rows are worked in garter stitch (2 rows with each color). Color C is the yellow mohair and Color D is the lightest speckle in the sample shawl.

Row 1 (RS): Using C, k3, *yo, k1, (yo, k2tog) twice, repeat from * to last 5 sts, yo, k2tog, yo k3. 543 sts. Turn to work WS.
Row 2 (WS): K3, yo, k to last 3 sts, yo, k3. 545 sts. Turn to work RS.

Row 3 (RS): Using D, k3, yo, k to last 3 sts, yo, k3.
Row 4 (WS): Using D, k3, yo, k to last 3 sts, yo, k3.
Row 5 (RS): Using C, k3, yo, k to last 3 sts, yo, k3.
Row 6 (WS): Using C, k3, yo, k to last 3 sts, yo, k3.

Repeat Rows 3-6 twice more. 569 sts. Break color C.

SECTION 2 - Both Sizes
The small size uses color C (blue speckle). The Large size uses color D (white speckle).
Row 1 (RS): Using C [D], k3, yo, k5, *k1, yo, ssk, k7, k2tog, yo, repeat from * to last 9 sts, k6, yo, k3. 415 [571] sts.
Row 2 (WS): K3, yo, k to last 3 sts, yo, k3. 417 [573] sts.

Row 3 (RS): K3, yo, k9, *yo, ssk, k5, k2tog, yo, k3, repeat from * to last 9 sts, k6, yo, k3. 419 [575] sts.
Row 4 (WS): K3, yo, k to last 3 sts, yo, k3. 421 [577] sts.

Row 5 (RS): K3, yo, k12, *yo, ssk, k3, k2tog, yo, k5, repeat from * to last 10 sts, k7, yo, k3. 423 [579] sts.
Row 6 (WS): K3, yo, k to last 3 sts, yo, k3. 425 [581] sts.

Row 7 (RS): K3, yo, k15, *yo, ssk, k1, k2tog, yo, k7, repeat from * to last 11 sts, k8, yo, k3. 427 [583] sts.
Row 8 (WS): K3, yo, k to last 3 sts, yo, k3. 429 [585] sts.

Follow this video tutorial for the yarn over wrap technique in Row 9...
https://youtu.be/r1mNT8Nhsnw

Row 9 (RS): K3, yo, k13, *k into next stitch wrapping yarn around the needle 5 times, k4, yo, sk2p, yo, k4, repeat from * to last 17 sts,
k into next stitch wrapping yarn around the needle 5 times, k13, yo, k3.

Follow this video tutorial for the short row cluster technique in Row 10...
https://youtu.be/ZvBX4K8J7eM

This next row is written on several lines for visual clarity. You will make short row clusters when you reach the 5 yarn over wraps.

Row 10 (WS): K3, yo, k14,
*K1/p1 into first yo
K1/p1 into second yo
K1/p1 into third yo
K1/p1 into fourth yo
K1/p1/k1 into fifth yo (11 total stitches coming from the big hole)
Turn to RS. K11.
Turn to WS. K10.
Turn to RS. K9.
Turn to WS. K8.
Turn to RS. K7.
Turn to WS. K6.
Turn to RS. K5.
Turn to WS. K4.
Turn to RS. K3.
Turn to WS. K2.
Turn to RS. K1.
Turn to WS. Sl1 purl-wise.
WS: continue to work WS as follows, (yo, k1) 6 times, k10, repeat from * to last 6 sts, k3, yo k3. 1011 [1341] sts.

Continue with SECTION 3 for Small Size only or skip to SECTION 3 for Large Size only.

SECTION 3 - Small Size only
Row 1 (RS): Using A, k3, yo, k14, *k13, (yo, k1) 6 times, yo, k3, sk2p, k3, yo, repeat from * to last 36 sts, k13, (yo, k1) 6 times, k14, yo, k3. 1217 sts.
Row 2 (WS): K3, yo, k to last 3 sts, yo, k3. 1219 sts.

Row 3 (RS): Using C, k3, yo, k15, *k27, yo, k2, sk2p, k2, yo, repeat from * to last 45 sts, k42, yo, k3. 1221 sts.

Row 4 (WS): K3, yo, k to last 3 sts, yo, k3. 1223 sts.

Row 5 (RS): Using A, k3, yo, k16, *k29, yo, k1, sk2p, k1, yo, repeat from * to last 48 sts, k45, yo, k3. 1225 sts.
Row 6 (WS): K3, yo, k to last 3 sts, yo, k3. 1227 sts.

Row 7 (RS): Using C, k3, yo, k17, *k31, yo, sk2p, yo, repeat from * to last 51 sts, k47, yo, k3.
1229 sts.
Row 8 (WS): K3, yo, k to last 3 sts, yo, k3. 1231 sts. Break color C.

Skip to FINISHING instructions.

SECTION 3 - Large Size only
Row 1 (RS): Using C, k3, yo, k11, *k16, (yo, k1) 6 times, k3, sk2p, repeat from * to last 36 sts, k16, (yo, k1) 6 times, k14, yo, k3. 1533 sts
Row 2 (WS): K3, yo, k to last 3 sts, yo, k3. 1535 sts.

Row 3 (RS): Using D, k3, yo, k17, *k23, sk2p 3 times, repeat from * to last 43 sts, k40, yo, k3. 1261 sts.
Row 4 (WS): K3, yo, k to last 3 sts, yo, k3.1263 sts. Break color D.

Row 5 (RS): Using C, k3, yo, k19, *k23, sk2p, repeat from * to last 45 sts, k42, yo, k3.
Row 6 (WS): K3, yo, k to last 3 sts, yo, k3.

FINISHING - Both Sizes
Using color A [C], BO all sts on the next RS row using a picot bind off as follows, *cast on 3 sts using the cable cast on method, (k2tog tbl, slip stitch onto left needle) 7 times, repeat from * until all sts are bound off. Break yarn, weave in ends, and block the finished shawl.

Large Size
4 colors

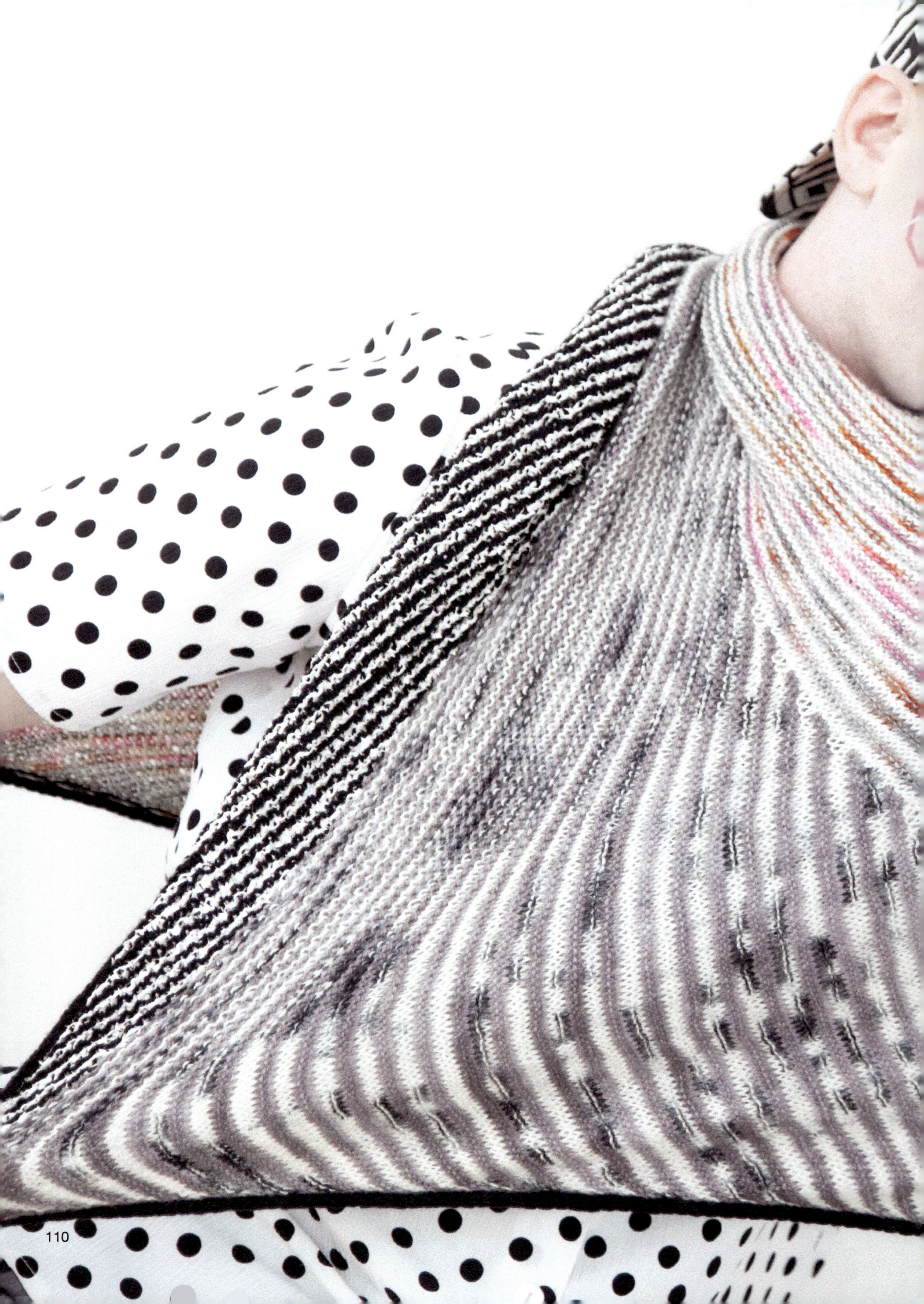

GARTER BREEZE

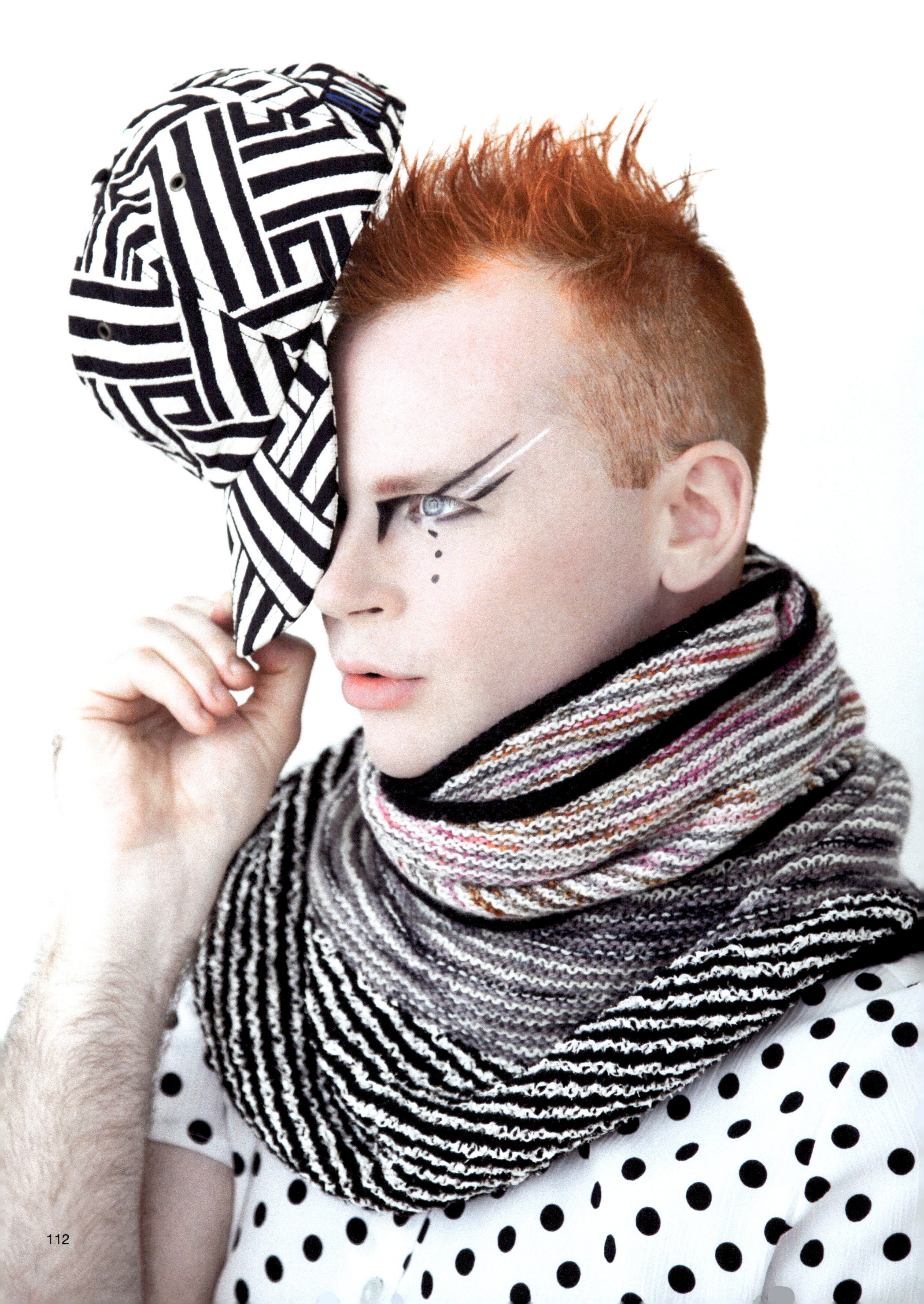

GARTER BREEZE

This simple garter stitch shawl is composed of three sections that grow with short rows and increases. Choose fingering weight yarns to knit stripes in each section or create a mixture of solid and striped sections. The simple shape is yours to paint with yarn colors! An I-cord border finishes the shawl for a final color pop.

Finished Measurements: 92" / 234cm wingspan length, 15" / 38cm wide. Measurements taken after blocking.

Yarn: Fingering weight

Shown in: Black & White Version
BC Garn Semilla (100% Wool; 176yds / 161m per 50g ball)
Color A - 02 Black

Bart & Francis Alien Fantasy (Goldfish, linen, cotton, latex; 109yds / 100m per 50g cone)
Color B - White

Malabrigo Finito (100% Merino; 200yds / 183m per 50g skein)
Color C - Plomo (gray)

Miss Babs Northumbria Fingering - BFL (100% Wool; 437yds / 400m per 100g skein)
Color D - Ansel (black & white), Color F - Deep Sea Jellyfish (variegated gray/pink/orange)

Madelinetosh Tosh Merino Light (100% Wool; 420yds / 384m per 115g skein)
Color E - Antler

Pink & Blue Version
La Bien Aimée Merino Singles (400ys / 366m per 100g skein)
Color A & B - Pandemonium
Color C - Sea Glass
Color D - Liesl
Color E - Parchment
Color F - Interstellar

Yardage: Color A - 160yds / 146m (Section 1 & I-cord border)
Color B - 60 yds / 55m (Section 1)
Color C - 145yds / 133m (Section 2)
Color D - 145yds / 133m (Section 2)
Color E - 310yds / 283m (Section 3)
Color F - 310yds / 283m (Section 3)

If you wish to use an extra color for the I-cord, it uses approximately 100yds / 91m.

Needles: 40" US 5 / 3.75mm circular

Notions: Tapestry needle

Gauge: 20 sts & 52 rows = 4" / 10cm in garter stitch

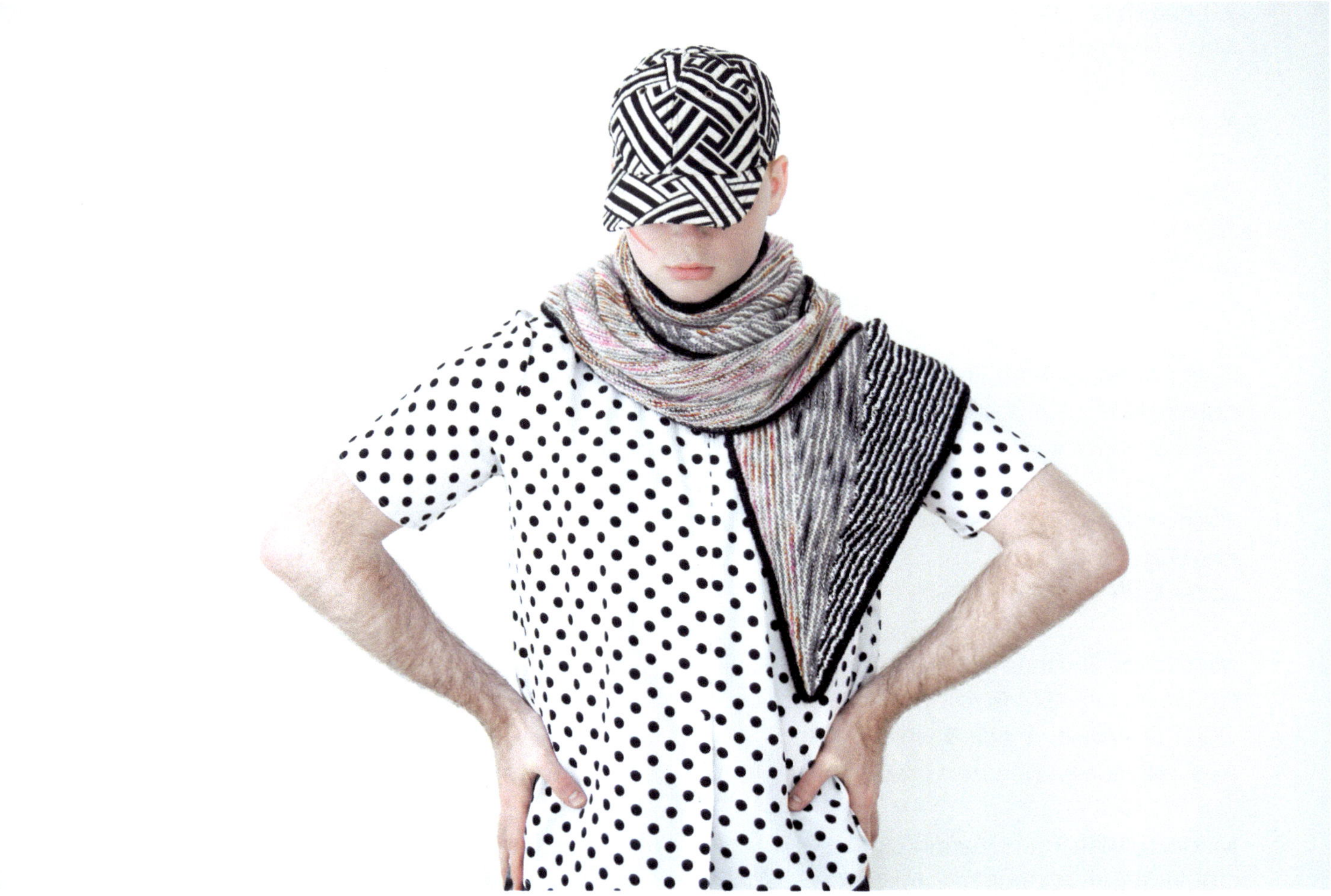

INSTRUCTIONS

SECTION 1
Using A, CO 120 sts.

Next Row (WS): K to last st, sl1 wyif.

Row 1 (RS): Using B, kfb, k to last 3 sts, turn to work WS.
Row 2 (WS): K to last st, sl1 wyif.

Row 3 (RS): Using A, kfb, k to 3 sts before last turn, turn to work WS.
Row 4 (WS): K to last st, sl1 wyif.

Repeat last 2 rows 56 more times while alternating colors A & B for 2 rows each. There should be 59 total garter ridges. 178 sts. Break colors A & B.

SECTION 2
Row 1 (RS): Using C, kfb, k to last st while closing the short row gaps, sl1 wyif.
Row 2 (WS): K to last st, sl1 wyif.

Row 3 (RS): Using D, kfb, k to last 3 sts, turn to work WS.
Row 4 (WS): K to last st, sl1 wyif.

Row 5 (RS): Using C, kfb, k to 3 sts before last turn, turn to work WS.
Row 6 (WS): K to last st, sl1 wyif.

Repeat last 2 rows 85 more times while striping colors C & D for 2 rows each. There should be 44 garter ridges of each color. 266 sts. Break colors C & D.

SECTION 3
Row 1 (RS): Using E, kfb, k to last st while closing the short row gaps, sl1 wyif.
Row 2 (WS): K to last st, sl1 wyif.

Row 3 (RS): Using F, kfb, k to last 3 sts, turn to work WS.
Row 4 (WS): K to last st, sl1 wyif.

Row 5 (RS): Using E, kfb, k to 3 sts before last turn, turn to work WS.
Row 6 (WS): K to last st, sl1 wyif.

Repeat last 2 rows 129 more times while striping colors E & F for 2 rows each. There should be 66 garter ridges of each color. 398 sts. Break colors E & F.

BORDER
The border uses approximately 100yds / 91m.

Next Row (RS): Using D or your color of choice for the I-cord border, kfb, k all sts while closing the short row gaps, pick up and k1 st into each selvedge st around the corner where all 3 colors meet, pick up and k1 st into each CO st, pick up and (k4, m1) along the increase edge. For this increase edge pick up, pick up and k1 st into each selvedge st 4 times, then m1 (make 1) using the backwards loop cast on. This increase will ensure your edge is not too tight.

You should now have sts around the entire perimeter of the shawl.

CO 3 sts using the cable CO technique. BO all sts using an I-cord BO as follows, *k2, k2tog tbl, place 3 sts back onto left needle, repeat from * until all sts are bound off.

FINISHING
Weave in ends and block the finished scarf to smooth the fabric.

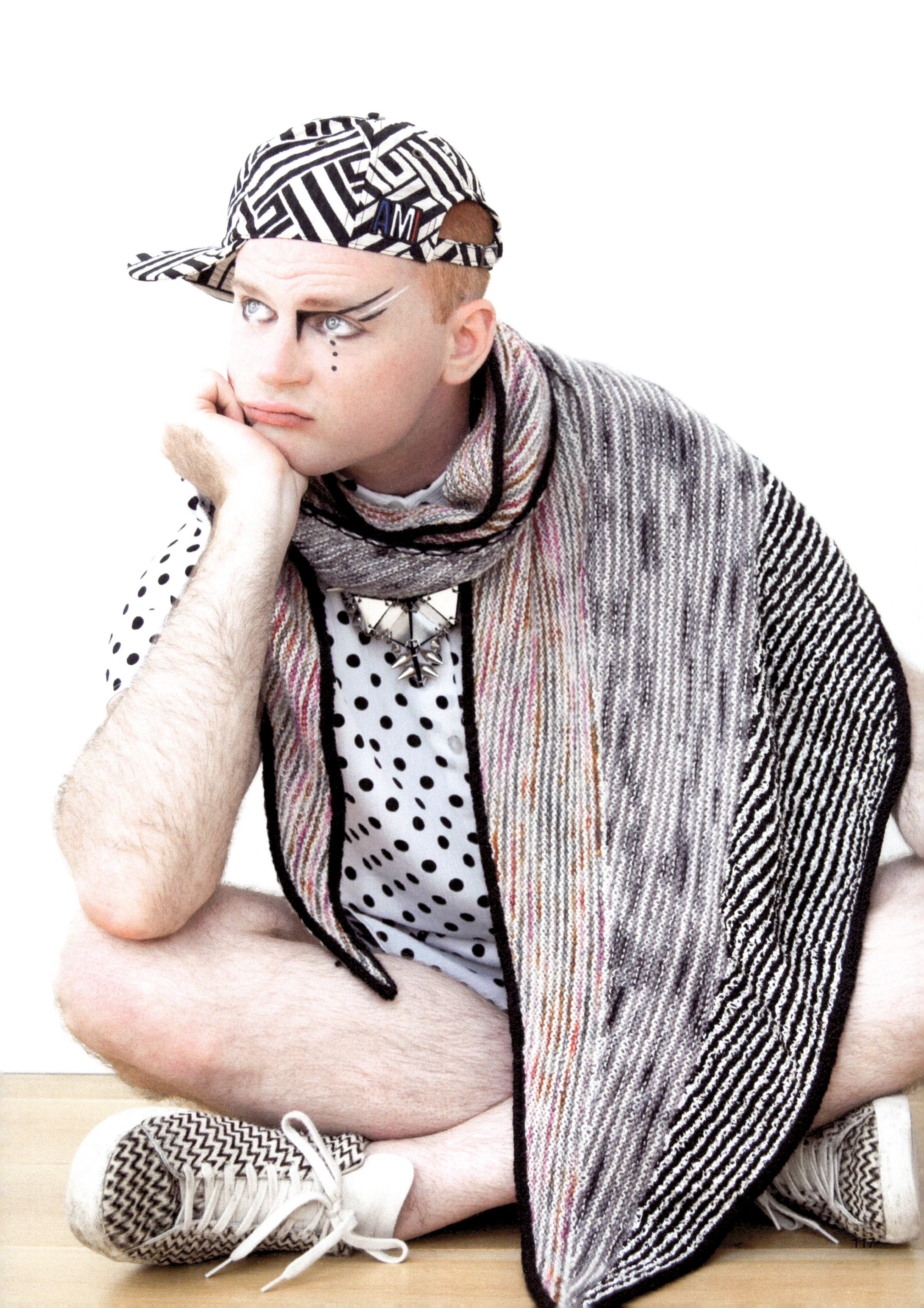
AMI

La Bien Aimée
Merino Singles

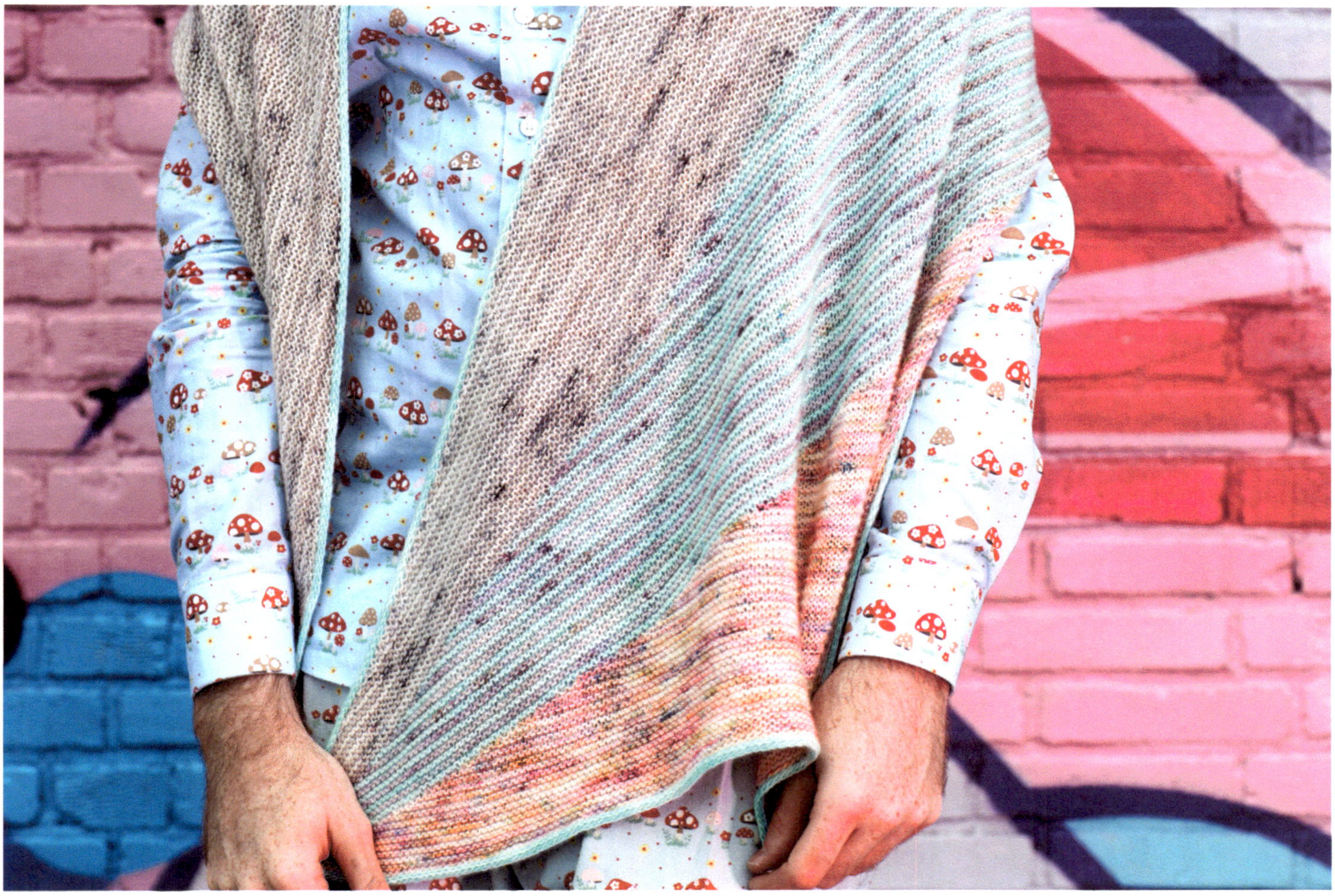

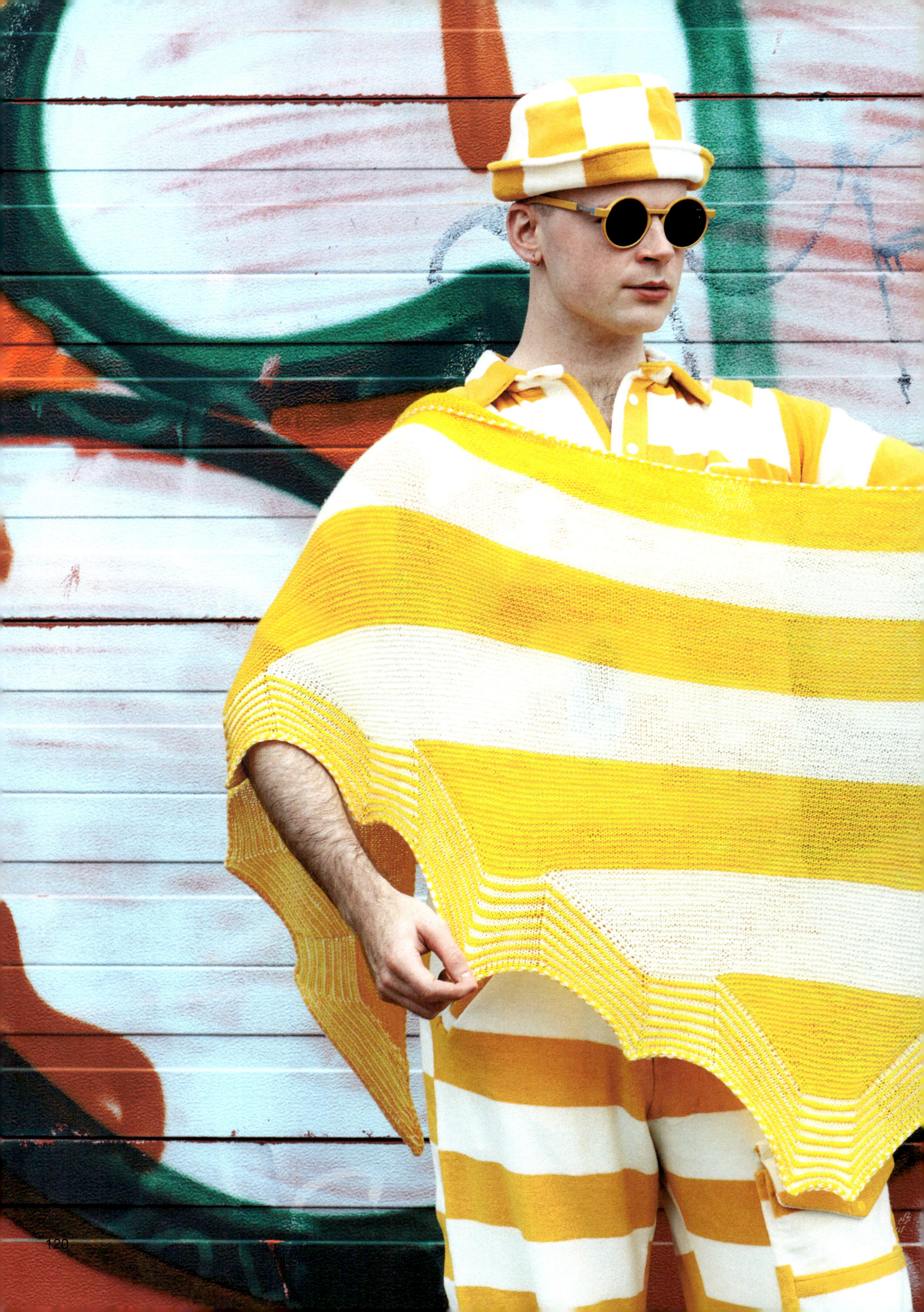

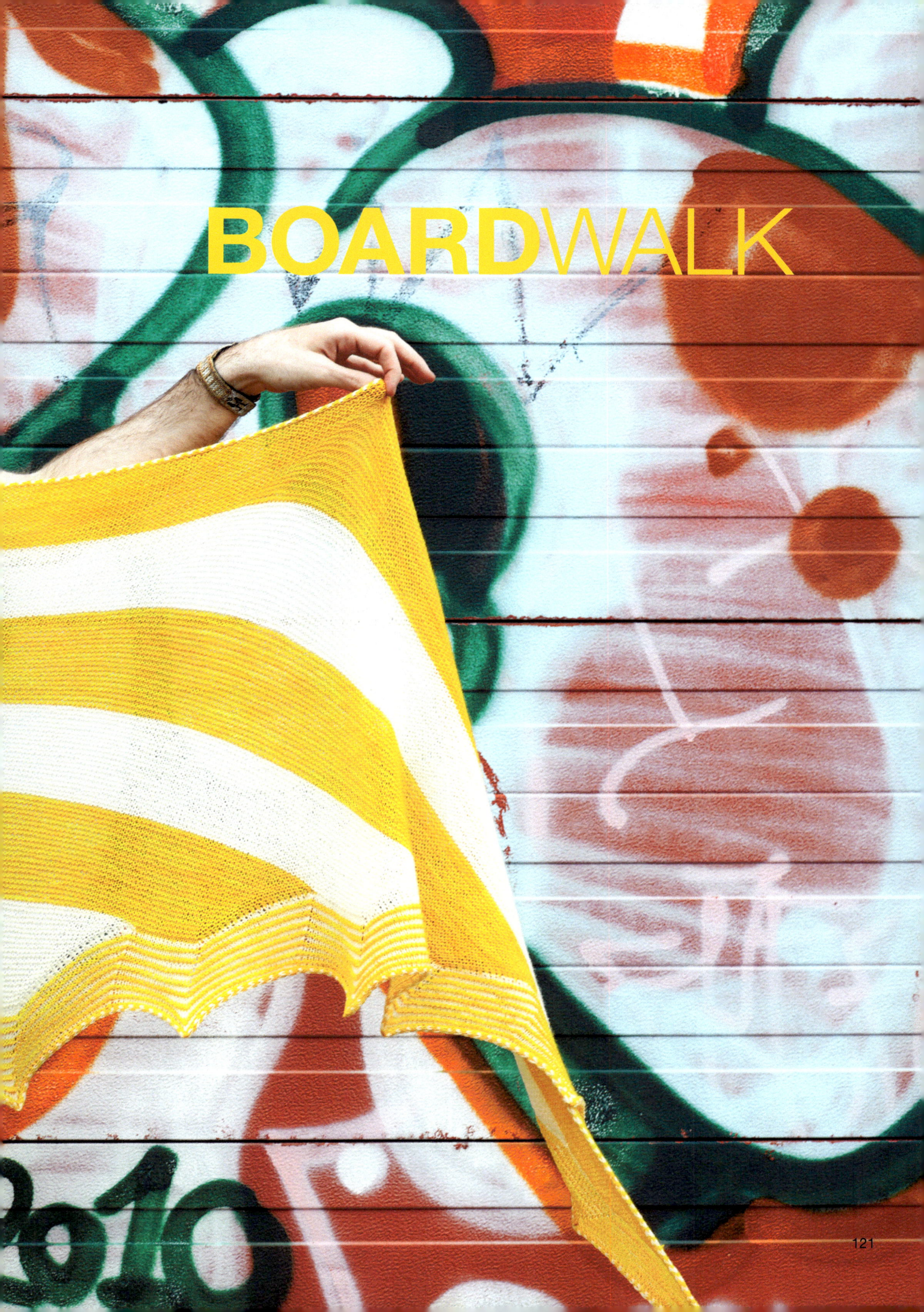

BOARDWALK

BOARDWALK

This large shawl begins at the bottom with small trapezoid shapes in garter stitch. Increases expand the trapezoids as they change color. The jagged border is picked up and knit with thin stockinette and garter ridge stripes. An I-cord edge frames the entire shape. Choose two colors for a strong graphic effect or change colors in every section using your stash yarns.

Sizes: Small [Medium, Large]

Finished Measurements: 96 [110, 120]" / 244 [279, 305]cm wingspan from tip to tip, 28 [31, 34]" / 71 [79, 86]cm along center point from CO to BO edge. Measurements taken after blocking. White/yellow stripes shown in large size.

Yarn: Fingering weight

Shown in: Small Size (5 trapezoids)
Hedgehog Fibres Sock Yarn
Color A - Where's my Bike?
Color B - Skinny Dip
Color C - Fool's Gold

Medium Size (6 trapezoids)
Hedgehog Fibres Sock Yarn in Typewriter (Trapezoid 1), Where's My Bike? (Trapezoid 2), Boombox (Trapezoid 3), & Oracle (Border)
Garnstories Merino Supersoft in Polar (Trapezoid 4), Gib Mir Saures (Trapezoid 5), & Neptun's Segen (Trapezoid 6)
Madelinetosh Tosh Merino Light in Neon Lime (Border)
Each trapezoid is a different colored speckle. Hedgehog Oracle and Madelinetosh Neon Lime are striped for the border.

Large Size (7 trapezoids)
Hedgehog Fibres Sock Yarn (90% Merino, 10% Nylon; 437yds / 400m per 100g skein)
Color A - Egg Yolk
Color B - Natural undyed

Yardage: Small Size (5 trapezoids)
Color A - 600yds / 549m
Color B - 410yds / 375m
The pattern is written for colors A & B but if you are working a 3-color small size, color A is split between color A and color C. You only need 1 ball of each color for a 3-color version.

Small Size 3-color version
Color A (trapezoids) - 400yds / 366m
Color B (trapezoids and section 2 garter ridge stripes) - 410yds / 375m
Color C (section 2 gold stockinette stripes) - 230yds / 210m

Medium Size (6 trapezoids)
Color A - 650yds / 594m
Color B - 700yds / 640m

Large Size (7 trapezoids shown in yellow & white)
Color A - 870yds / 796m
Color B - 700yds / 640m

Needles: 47" US 4 / 3.5mm circular

Notions: 26 stitch markers, tapestry needle

Gauge: 22 sts & 52 rows = 4" / 10cm in garter st

Pattern Notes: The pattern starts with the thick trapezoid stripes. The large sample size shows all 7 wide stripes. The medium size features 6 stripes and the small features 5 stripes. The two-row striped chevron border is customizable. You can knit as few or as many stripes as you like until you bind off.

Medium Size
8 colors

Small Size
3 colors

INSTRUCTIONS
SECTION 1

Trapezoid 1
Using A, CO 18 sts.

Next Row (WS): K17, sl1 wyif.

Row 1 (RS): Kfb, k to last st, sl1 wyif.
Row 2 (WS): Kfb, k to last st, sl1 wyif.

Repeat last 2 rows 18 more times. There should be 20 garter ridges. 56 sts.

Trapezoid 2
Row 1 (RS): Using B, CO 17 sts using the cable CO method, k all sts.
Row 2 (WS): CO 17 sts using the cable CO method, k to last st, sl1 wyif.

Row 3 (RS): Kfb, k to last st, sl1 wyif.
Row 4 (WS): Kfb, k to last st, sl1 wyif.

Repeat last 2 rows 18 more times. There should be 20 color B garter ridges. 128 sts. Break color B.

Trapezoid 3
Row 1 (RS): Using A, CO 17 sts using the cable CO method, k all sts.
Row 2 (WS): CO 17 sts using the cable CO method, k to last st, sl1 wyif.

Row 3 (RS): Kfb, k to last st, sl1 wyif.
Row 4 (WS): Kfb, k to last st, sl1 wyif.

Repeat last 2 rows 18 more times. There should be 20 color A garter ridges. 200 sts. Break color A.

Continue by following Small, Medium, or Large Size instructions.

Small Size
Work Trapezoids 2 & 3 once more. There should be 3 color A trapezoids and 2 color B trapezoids. 344 sts.
Break yarn and place all sts onto waste yarn or spare circular needle.

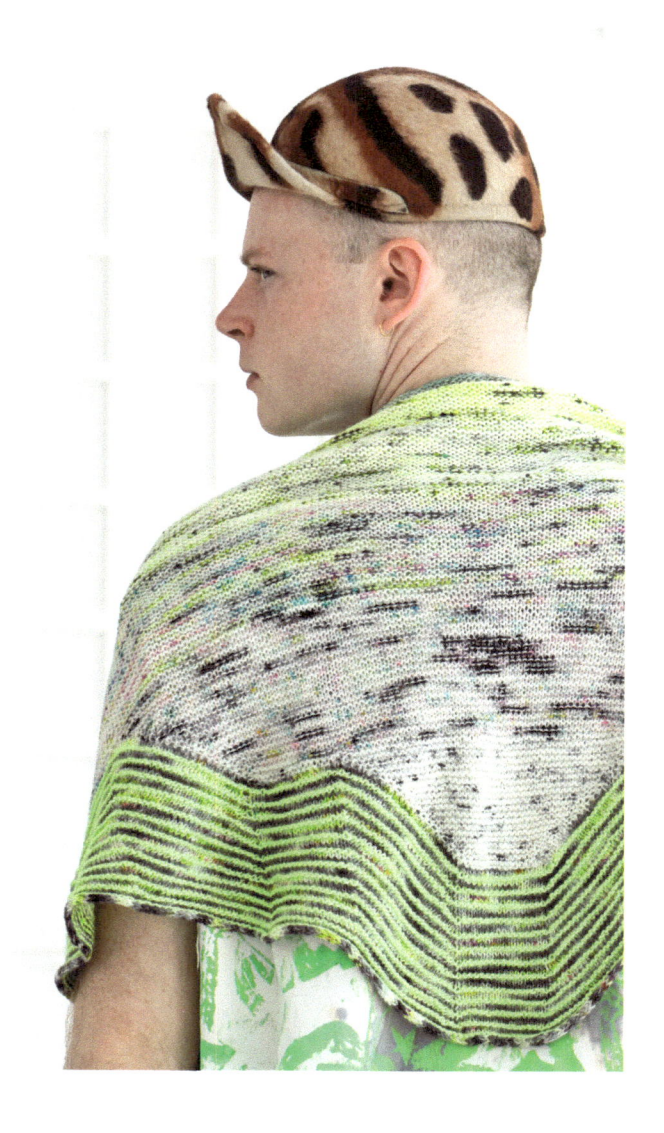

Medium Size
Work Trapezoids 2 & 3 once more then repeat Trapezoid 2 once more. There should be 3 color A trapezoids and 3 color B trapezoids. 416 sts.
Break yarn and place all sts onto waste yarn or spare circular needle.

Large Size
Work Trapezoids 2 & 3 twice more. There should be 4 color A trapezoids and 3 color B trapezoids. 488 sts.
Break yarn and place all sts onto waste yarn or spare circular needle.

SECTION 2

Begin picking up sts into the Trapezoid #5 [6, 7] color A selvedge.

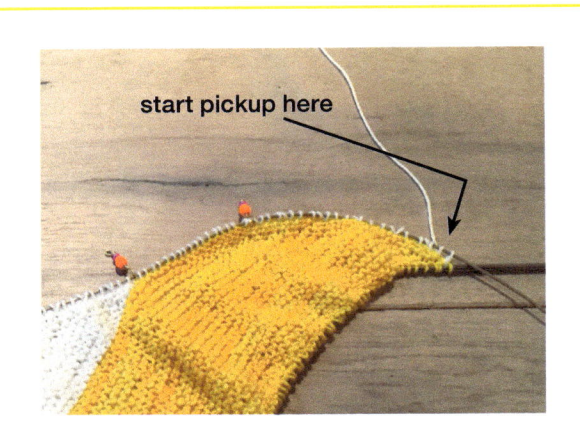

Note: If you are working a 3-color version and you are introducing your third color in the border now, begin this pick up row with color C instead of color B. You will alternate colors C & B for 2-row stripes until the border reaches your desired length.

Using B and with RS facing, *(pick up and k3, m1) 6 times, pick up and k2, pm, pick up and k16 from CO edge, pm, repeat from * 4 [5, 6] more times. You should now be at the bottom edge by the original color A cast on. *(Pickup and k3, m1) 6 times, k2, pm, pick up and k16, pm, repeat from * 3 [4, 5] more times, *(pick up and k3, m1), k2, turn work WS.

Next Row (WS): P to last st, sl1 wyif.

Row 1 (RS): Using A, kfb, *k to m, M1R, slm, k16, slm, ssk, repeat from * 3 [4, 5] more times, k to m, M1R, slm, **k16, slm, M1L, k to 2 sts before m, k2tog, slm, repeat from ** 3 [4, 5] more times, k16, slm, M1L, k to last st, sl1 wyif.
Row 2 (WS): Kfb, k to last st, sl1 wyif.
Row 3 (RS): Using B, kfb, *k to m, M1R, slm, k16, slm, ssk, repeat from * 3 [4, 5] more times, k to m, M1R, slm, **k16, slm, M1L, k to 2 sts before m, k2tog, slm, repeat from ** 3 [4, 5] more times, k16, slm, M1L, k to last st, sl1 wyif.
Row 4 (WS): Kfb, p to last st, sl1 wyif.

Repeat last 4 rows 6 more times. If you have more yarn and wish to make a larger border, continue repeating Rows 1-4 until the border reaches your desired size. Break colors A & B.

Next Row (RS): Using A, pick up and (k3, m1) along SECTION 2 selvedge until all sts are picked up. Kfb, *k to m, M1R, slm, k16, slm, ssk, repeat from * 3 [4, 5] more times, k to m, M1R, slm, **k16, slm, M1L, k to 2 sts before m, k2tog, slm, repeat from ** 3 [4, 5] more times, k16, slm, M1L, k to end of row. Pick up and (k3, m1) along SECTION 2 selvedge. Turn to work WS.

Next Row (WS): K all sts.

Continue to bind off with both colors for a striped I-cord bind off or bind off all sts using color A for a solid edge. The I-cord bind off requires approximately 65 [75, 80] yds / 59 [69, 73]m total.

Striped I-cord Bind Off
Using A, CO 3 sts using the cable CO method. *Using A, k2, k2tog tbl, slip 3 sts onto left needle. Using B, k2, k2tog tbl, slip 3 sts onto left needle. Repeat from * alternating colors A & B until all sts are bound off around the entire perimeter of the shawl. Break yarn and pull it through the last 3 sts.

FINISHING

Weave in ends. Block finished shawl to smooth the fabric and exaggerate the points.

Large Size
2 colors

127

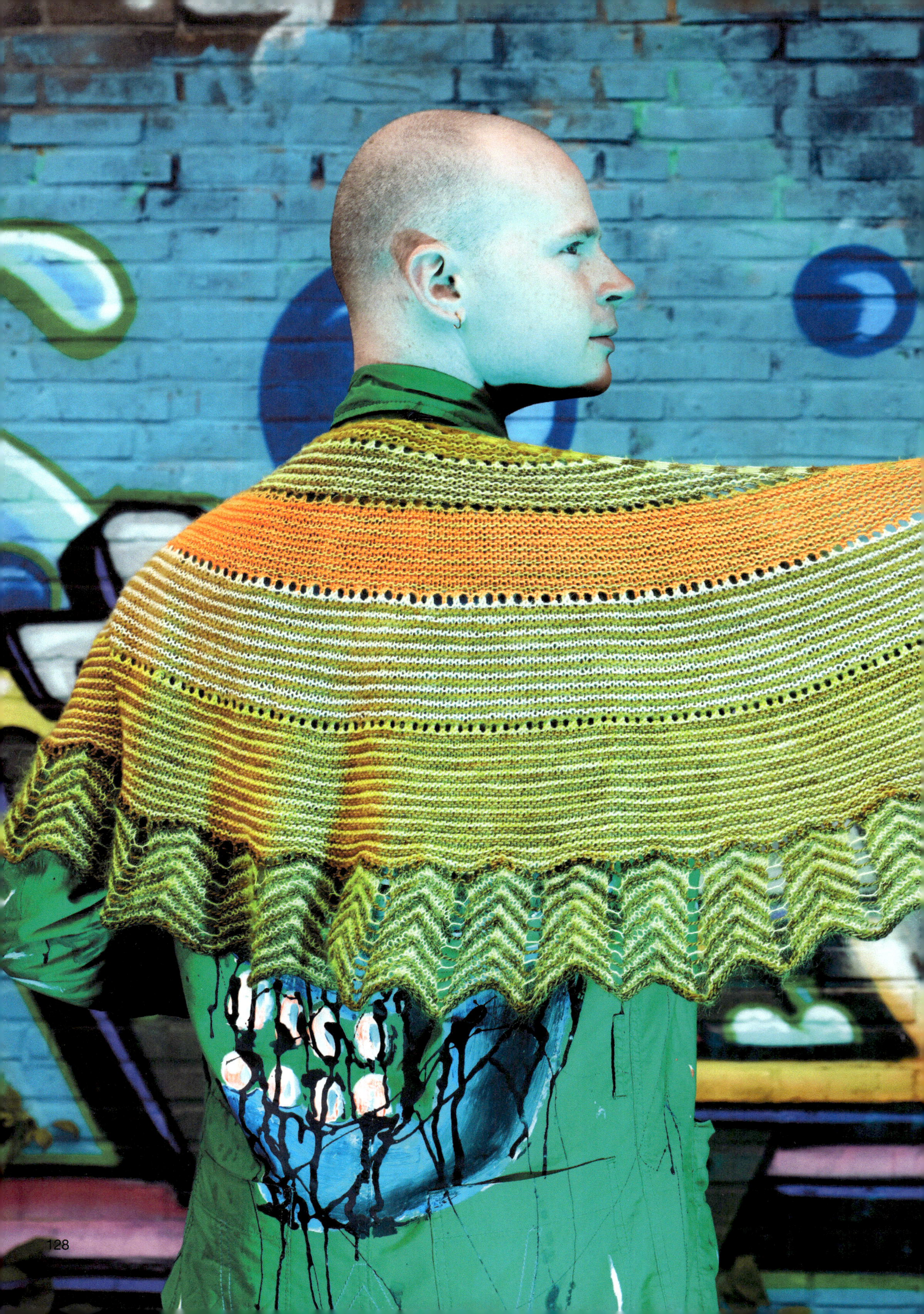

HOLEY
CHEVRONS

Large Size
12 colors

HOLEY CHEVRONS

This top-down shawl is knit with garter stitch stripes while yarn over holes expand the fabric into a semi-circle. A final chevron border gives the shawl a scalloped edge. The small size is knit with 2 colors while the large size features 12 shades of yellow and orange.

Sizes: Small [Large]

Finished Measurements: 60 [102]" / 152 [259]cm wingspan, 14 [23]" / 36 [58]cm from CO to BO edge. Measurements taken after blocking.

Yarn: Fingering weight

Shown in: Small Size Cream Version
La Bien Aimée Merino Singles (100% Merino Wool; 400yds / 366m per 100g skein)
Color A - Paisley
La Bien Aimée Mohair Silk (70% Mohair, 30% Silk; 546yds / 499m per 50g skein)
Color B - Natural White

Small Size Blue Version
La Bien Aimée Merino Singles
Color A - Wee Rainbow on a Vespa
La Bien Aimée Mohair Silk
Color B - Vespa

Large Size Orange/Yellow Version
Various fingering weight yarns including...
Madelinetosh Tosh Merino Light
Malabrigo Finito
A Verb for Keeping Warm Floating

Yardage: Small Size
Color A - 270yds / 247m
Color B - 260yds / 238m

Large Size
A1 - 5yds / 5m
B1 - 5yds / 5m
A2 - 20yds / 18m
B2 - 20yds / 18m
A3 - 50yds / 46m
B3 - 50yds / 46m
A4 - 90yds / 82m
B4 - 90yds / 82m
A5 - 160yds / 146m
B5 - 160yds / 146m
A6 - 150yds / 137m
B6 - 150yds / 137m
Color A Total: 475yds / 434m
Color B Total: 475yds / 434m

Needles: 40" US 6 / 4mm circular

Notions: Tapestry needle

Gauge: 20 sts & 40 rows = 4" / 10cm in garter stitch

Pattern Notes: Instructions are written using colors A & B with notes where to change colors if you're knitting the large size with 12 colors. For a two-color version, use the same color A & B throughout the entire project.

INSTRUCTIONS
SECTION 1
Using A, CO 3 sts. K7 rows.
At the end of last row, do not turn to work other side, rotate piece 90 degrees clockwise so that you are looking at the long side of the garter rectangle. Pick up and k3 sts in the purl bump of each garter ridge. Rotate piece another 90 degrees. Pick up and k3 sts along the CO edge. 9 sts. Turn to work WS row.

Next Row (WS): K3, yo, k3, yo, k3. 11 sts.
Next Row (RS): Using B, k3, (yo, k1) 6 times, k2. 17 sts.
Next Row (WS): K3, yo, k to last 3 sts, yo, k3. 19 sts.

Row 1 (RS): Using A, k3, yo, k to last 3 sts, yo, k3.
Row 2 (WS): K3, yo, k to last 3 sts, yo, k3.

Repeat last 2 rows 4 more times while working 2-row stripes with colors B & A. 39 sts. For a multi-striped version, break colors A1 & B1 and replace them with A2 & B2.

Row 11 (RS): Using B, k3, (yo, k1, yo, k2tog) 11 times, yo, k3. 51 sts.
Row 12 (WS): K3, yo, k to last 3 sts, yo, k3. 53 sts.

Repeat Rows 1 & 2 9 more times while working 2-row stripes with colors A & B. 89 sts. For a multi-striped version, break colors A2 & B2 and replace them with A3 & B3.

Row 31 (RS): Using B, k3, (yo, k1, yo, k2tog) 27 times, yo, k2tog, yo, k3. 117 sts.
Row 32 (WS): K3, yo, k to last 3 sts, yo, k3. 119 sts.

Repeat Rows 1 & 2 13 more times while working 2-row stripes with colors A & B. 171 sts. For a multi-striped version, break colors A3 & B3 and replace them with A4 & B4.

Row 59 (RS): Using B, k3, (yo, k1, yo, k2tog) 55 times, yo, k3. 227 sts.
Row 60 (WS): K3, yo, k to last 3 sts, yo, k3. 229 sts.

Repeat Rows 1 & 2 17 more times while working 2-row stripes with colors A & B. 297 sts. For a multi-striped version break colors A4 & B4 and replace them with A5 & B5. Continue with Small Size or skip to Large Size instructions.

Small Size Only
Row 95 (RS): Using B, k3, (yo, k1, yo, k2tog) 94 times, (yo, k1) 9 times, yo, k3. 401 sts.
Row 96 (WS): K3, yo, k to last 3 sts, yo, k3. 403 sts.

SECTION 2 - Small Size Only
Row 1 (RS): Using A, k3, yo, k3, pm, ssk, k6 (yo twice, k6, SK2P, k6) 25 times, yo twice, k6, k2tog, pm, k3, yo, k3.
Row 2 (WS): K3, yo, k to m, slm, k7, (k1/p1 into double yo, k13) 25 times, k1/p1 into double yo, k7, slm, k to last 3 sts, yo, k3.

Row 3 (RS): Using B, k3, yo, k to m, slm, ssk, k6, (yo twice, k6, SK2P, k6) 25 times, yo twice, k6, k2tog, slm, k to last 3 sts, yo, k3.
Row 4 (WS): K3, yo, k to m, slm, k7, (k1/p1 into double yo, k13) 25 times, k1/p1 into double yo, k7, slm, k to last 3 sts, yo, k3.

Row 5 (RS): Using A, k3, yo, k to m, slm, ssk, k6, (yo twice, k6, SK2P, k6) 25 times, yo twice, k6, k2tog, slm, k to last 3 sts, yo, k3.
Row 6 (WS): K3, yo, k to m, slm, k7, (k1/p1 into double yo, k13) 25 times, k1/p1 into double yo, k7, slm, k to last 3 sts, yo, k3.

Repeat Rows 3-6 8 more times. If you wish to make a larger border, continue repeating Rows 3-6 until the border is your desired size. Break color B. You will BO with color A. Skip to FINISHING instructions.

Large Size Only
Row 95 (RS): Using B, k3, (yo, k1, yo, k2tog) 97 times, yo, k3. 395 sts.
Row 96 (WS): K3, yo, k to last 3 sts, yo, k3. 397 sts.

Repeat Rows 1 & 2 21 more times while working 2-row stripes with colors A & B. 481 sts. For a multi-striped version, break colors A5 & B5 and replace them with A6 & B6.

Row 139 (RS): Using B, k3, (yo, k1, yo, k2tog) 158 times, yo, k1, yo, k3. 641 sts.
Row 140 (WS): K3, yo, k to last 3 sts, yo, k3. 643 sts.

SECTION 2 - Large Size Only
Row 1 (RS): Using A, k3, yo, k3, pm, ssk, k6 (yo twice, k6, SK2P, k6) 41 times, yo twice, k6, k2tog, pm, k3, yo, k3.
Row 2 (WS): K3, yo, k to m, slm, k7, (k1/p1 into double yo, k13) 41 times, k1/p1 into double yo, k7, slm, k to last 3 sts, yo, k3.

Row 3 (RS): Using B, k3, yo, k to m, slm, ssk, k6, (yo twice, k6, SK2P, k6) 41 times, yo twice, k6, k2tog, slm, k to last 3 sts, yo, k3.
Row 4 (WS): K3, yo, k to m, slm, k7, (k1/p1 into double yo, k13) 41 times, k1/p1 into double yo, k7, slm, k to last 3 sts, yo, k3.

Row 5 (RS): Using A, k3, yo, k to m, slm, ssk, k6, (yo twice, k6, SK2P, k6) 41 times, yo twice, k6, k2tog, slm, k to last 3 sts, yo, k3.
Row 6 (WS): K3, yo, k to m, slm, k7, (k1/p1 into double yo, k13) 41 times, k1/p1 into double yo, k7, slm, k to last 3 sts, yo, k3.

Repeat Rows 3-6 3 more times then repeat Rows 3 & 4 once more. Break color A.

FINISHING
Using color B, BO all sts loosely on following RS row as follows, (k2tog tbl, slip st to left needle) to end of row. Break yarn and pull it through the last stitch. Weave in ends and block the finished shawl.

Small Size
La Bien Aimée
Merino Singles & Mohair Silk

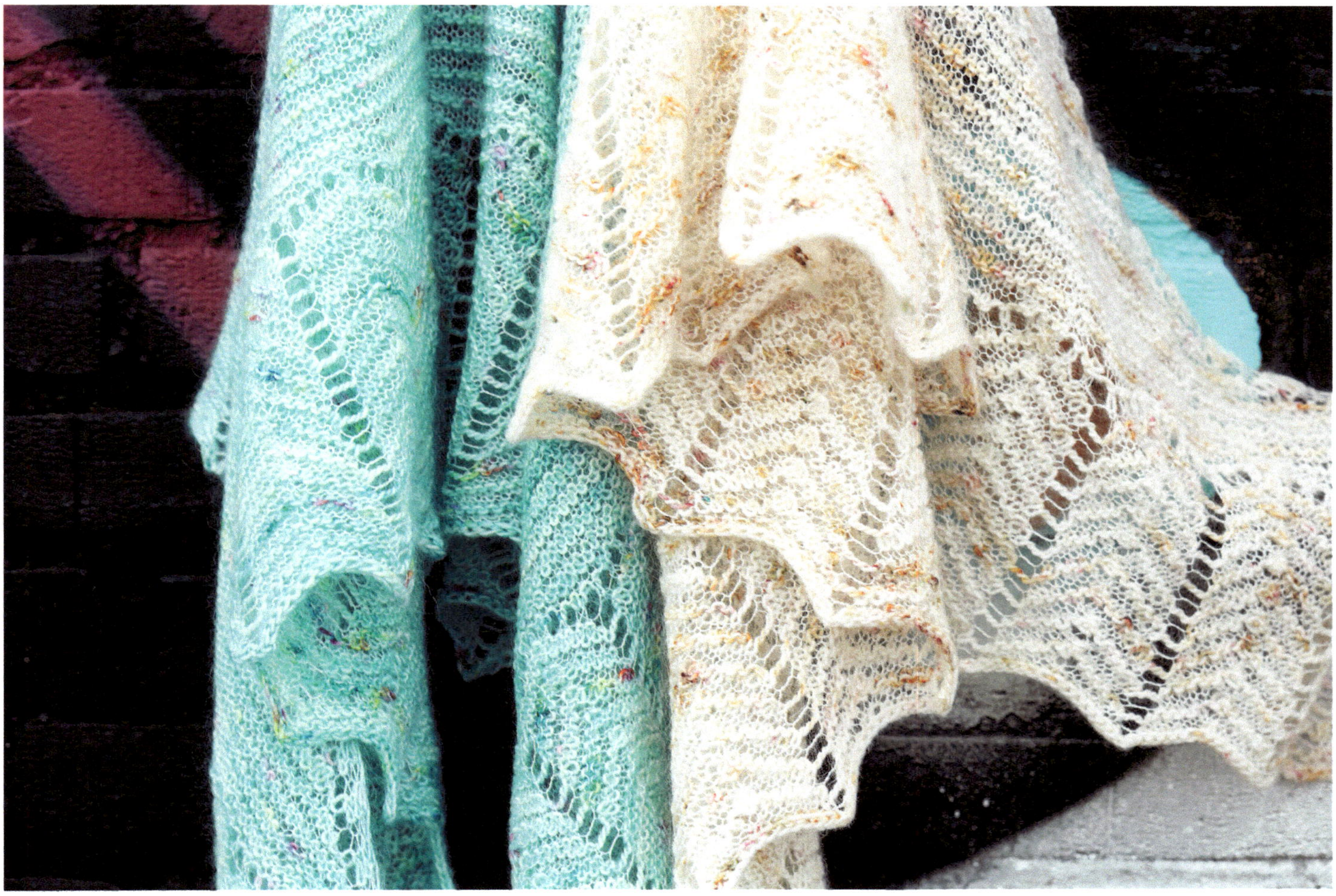

BRIOCHEVRON
WRAP

13

138

BRIOCHEVRON WRAP

Choose a colorful array of fingering weight yarns and knit this large wrap in two-color brioche. The main color is a black and white marled yarn from Woolfolk while bright color pops from Hedgehog Fibres decorate the striped background. Increases and decreases form the graphic chevron lines and the fabric length is customizable.

Finished Measurements: 19" / cm wide, 80" / 203cm long. Measurements taken after blocking.

Yarn: Fingering weight

Shown in: MC - Woolfolk Sno (100% Merino Wool; 223yds / 204m per 50g skein) Color 1 + 15 Black & White
CC - Hedgehog Fibres Sock Yarn (90% Merino, 10% Nylon; 437yds / 400m per 100g skein)
CC sample stripes shown in Coral, Highlighter, Oracle, Harajuku, Hush, Electric, Boombox, Where's My Bike?, Envy, Fool's Gold, Night Ride, Jelly, Skinny Dip, Work it!, Typewriter, Pollen, Budgie, Brithday Cake, Vengeance, Oh Snap!, and a few one-of-a-kind Potluck and club colors.

Yardage: MC - 1300 yds / 1189m
CC - 1250yds / 1143m

The contrast color used small amounts of leftover sock yarn and mini skeins. The colorful stripes vary between 3 and 12 rows.

Needles: 24" US 4 / 3.5mm circular

Notions: Tapestry needle

Gauge: 24 sts & 20 rows = 4" / 10cm in two-color briochevron stitch

Pattern Notes: In two-color brioche stitch, two rows are worked for each counted row that appears on the face of the fabric. The first color is worked across the row and then the row is worked again using the second color. The next row is worked the same way, once across with the first color and worked again with the second color. When counting rows, count only the stitches going up on a knit column. For example, when you work 4 rows, count 4 knit column stitches, even though you will have worked 8 rows. 2 worked rows = 1 counted row.

When you put down your knitting and forget which color you just used and which color to use next, look at the color of the yo in the row just worked. That is the last color you used.

INSTRUCTIONS

Using MC, CO 3 sts, *slip 3 sts to left needle, k3, repeat from * 159 more times.

Set-Up Row 1 RS MC: Pick up and k159 sts along I-cord edge, pick up and k3 sts from CO edge. Do not turn, slide sts to work the same row with the other color. 165 sts.

Set-Up Row 1 RS CC: Using CC, sl3, (sl1yo, p1) to last 4 sts, sl1yo, sl3 wyif. Turn work.

Set-Up Row 2 WS MC: P3, (brp1, sl1yo) to last 4 sts, brp1, p3. Do not turn, slide sts to work the same row with the other color.

Set-Up Row 2 WS CC: CC is hanging in back, sl3, (sl1yo, brk1) to last 4 sts, sl1 yo, sl3 wyib. Turn work.

Row 1 RS MC: K3, *brkyobrk, sl1yo, (brk1, sl1yo) 5 times, brRsl dec, sl1yo, brLsl dec, sl1yo, (brk1, sl1yo) 5 times, brkyobrk, sl1yo, repeat from * 4 more times. On the last repeat, ignore the last sl1yo. K the last 3 sts. Do not turn, slide sts to work the same row with the other color.

Row 1 RS CC: CC is hanging in front, sl3, (sl1yo, brp1) to last 4 sts, sl1yo, sl3 wyif. Turn work.

Row 2 WS MC: P3, (brp1, sl1yo) to last 4 sts, brp1, p3. Do not turn, slide sts to work the same row with the other color.

Row 2 WS CC: CC is hanging in back, sl3, (sl1yo, brk1) to last 4 sts, sl1 yo, sl3 wyib. Turn work.

Repeat Rows 1 & 2 until work measures approximately 80" / 203cm ending with Row 2 WS CC.

FINISHING

Next Row RS MC: K3, (brk1, k1) to last 4 sts, brk1, k3. Turn to BO on the WS.

Reverse the order of the first three stitches and BO all sts with an I-cord BO as follows, *k2, k2tog tbl, repeat from * to last 3 sts, Graft the 6 total sts together.

Break yarn, weave in ends, and block the finished wrap.

141

142

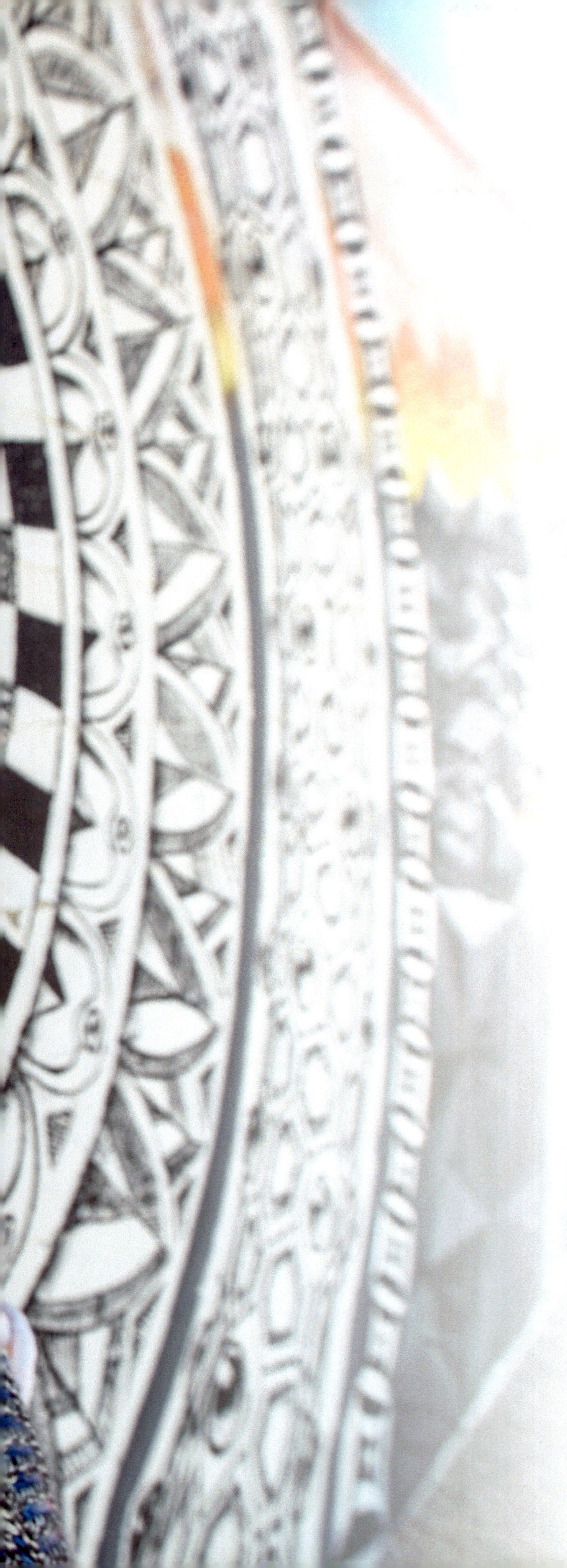

144

145

ABBREVIATIONS

BO: bind off

CC: contrast color

CO: cast on

k: knit

k2tog: knit two together

kfb: knit into front and back of stitch

m: marker

m1: (make one) increase 1 stitch using the backwards loop cast on method

M1L: (make one left) with left needle, lift strand between sts from the front, knit through the back loop

M1R: (make one right) with left needle, lift strand between sts from the back, knit through the front loop

MC: main color

p: purl

pm: place marker

RS: right side

SK2P: slip 1 knit-wise, knit 2 together, pass slipped stitch over

sl: slip (stitches are slipped purl-wise)

slm: slip marker

ssk: (slip slip knit) slip first stitch purl-wise, slip second stitch knit-wise, knit 2 together through back loop

st/s: stitch/es

tbl: through back loop

WS: wrong side

wyib: with yarn in back

wyif: with yarn in front

yf: yarn forward

yo: yarn over

BRIOCHE ABBREVIATIONS

brk: brioche knit also known as bark, knit the stitch (that was slipped in the previous row) together with its yarn over.

brkyobrk: Two stitches spring out of the center of one stitch with this increase. Work a brkyobrk as follows: brk1 (leave stitch on the needle), yo (yarn forward under needle then over needle to back), then brk1 into same stitch. 2 sts increased.

brp: brioche purl also known as burp, purl the stitch (that was slipped in the previous row) together with its yarn over.

brRsl dec: (a 2-stitch decrease that slants to the right, involving 3 sts) Slip the first stitch knit-wise, knit the next stitch, pass the slipped stitch over, place stitch on left hand needle and pass the following stitch over. Place st on right hand needle.

brLsl dec (2-stitch decrease that slants to the left, involving 3 sts) Slip the first stitch knit-wise, brk the following two stitches together, pass the slipped stitch over.

DC: dark color, use the dark colored yarn

LC: light color, use the light colored yarn

sl1yo following a k or brk st: (slip 1 yarn over) bring the working yarn under the needle to the front of the work, slip the next stitch purl-wise, then bring the yarn over the needle (and over the slipped stitch) to the back, in position to work the following stitch.
sl1yo following a p or brp st: (slip 1 yarn over) working yarn is already in front, slip the next stitch purl-wise, then bring the yarn over the needle (and over the slipped stitch), then to the front under the needle, into position to work the following stitch.

I highly recommend Nancy Marchant's classes and books on brioche knitting. Her online Craftsy class, *Explorations in Brioche Knitting*, offers excellent information on the intriguing brioche technique.

www.craftsy.com/ext/StephenWest_208_F

www.craftsy.com/brioche

www.briochestitch.com

PHOTO CREDITS
Makeup & Photography by Alexandra Feo
Pages 1-23, 52, 84, 91, 110-117, 148-151

Darren Smith
Pages 24-37, 44, 48-51, 54-60, 64, 68-72,
80-83, 86-88, 92-101, 107, 118-135, 140, 144

Jarrod Duncan
Pages 136-138, 141-143, 152

Lascoux Sébastien
Pages 38, 63, 66, 67,

John Smith
Pages 102-104, 109

Jonna Jolkin
Page 41

Kyli Kleven
Page 74

Styling and Modeling by Stephen West

SAMPLE KNITTERS

Aimee Osbourn-Gille - Dotted Rays
(La Bien Aimée sample)

Julie Dubreux - Garter Breeze
(blue/pink sample)

Gyorgi Suta - Vertices Unite (large),
Holey Chevrons (small), Boardwalk (medium)

Jacky van der Muelen - The Doodler
(purple sample), Boardwalk (small)

Anita Miresz - Dotted Rays
(blue/black/white/yellow sample)

All other samples knit by Stephen West

Thank you Malia, Lou, and Nancy for your constant support and friendship.

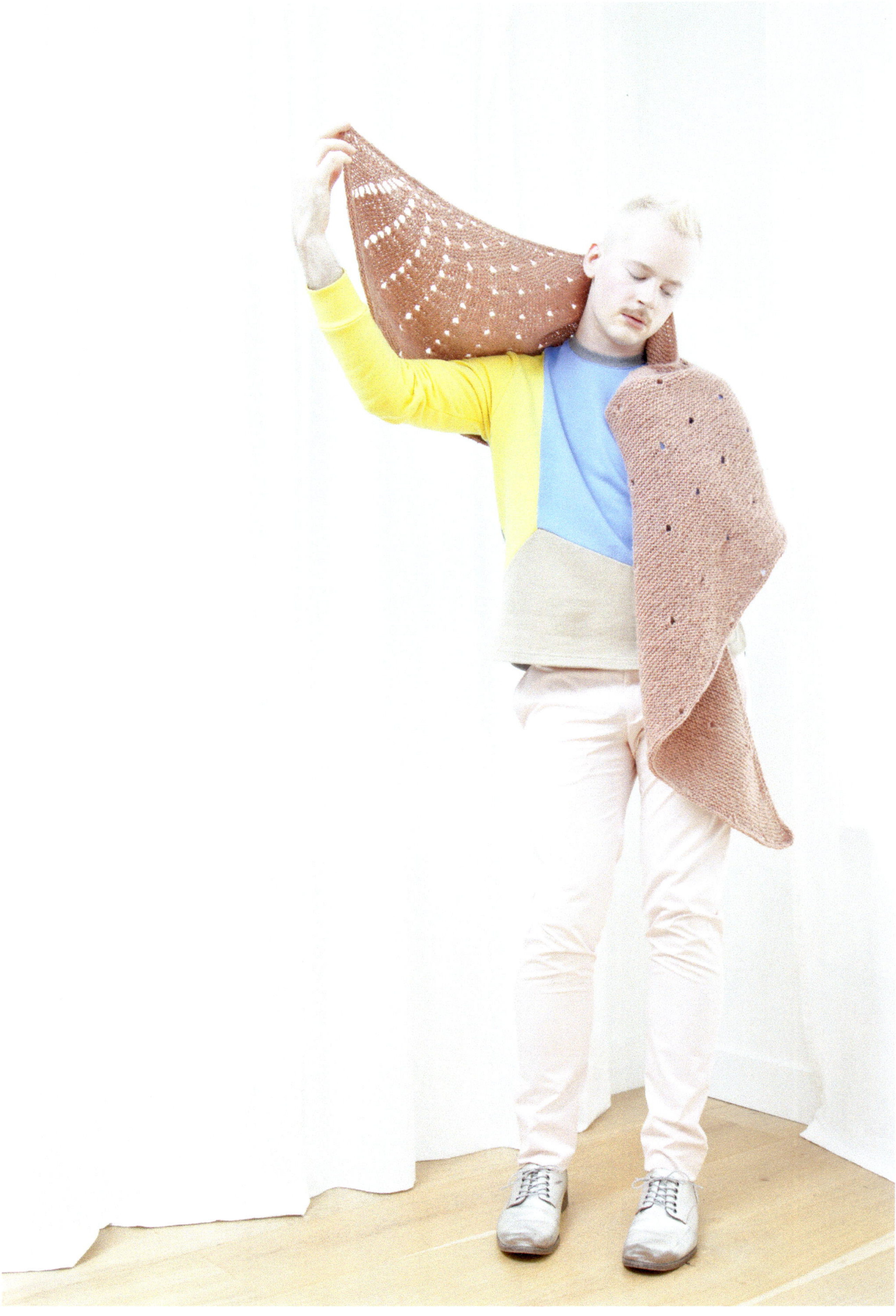

Dotted Rays
in Quince & Co Owl

CONTACT INFORMATION

Stephen West
www.westknits.com
www.stephenandpenelope.com

Customer support: support@westknits.eu

westknits

www.facebook.com/westknits

www.instagram.com/westknits

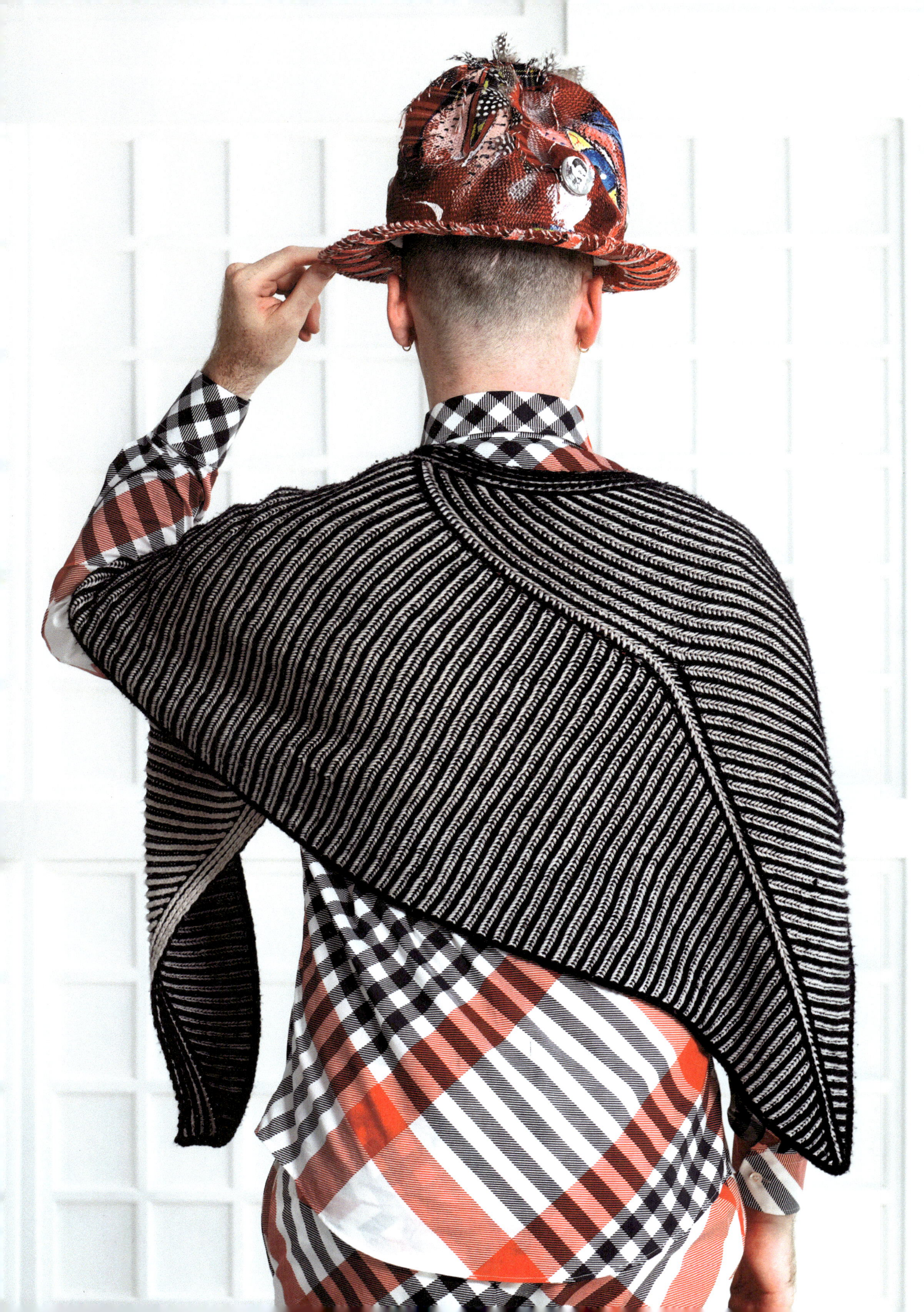